THE
MOON
SHOT
EFFECT

THE MOON SHOT EFFECT

Disrupting Business as Usual

LISA GOLDMAN & KATE PURMAL

with ANNE JANZER

WYNNEFIELD BUSINESS PRESS

THE MOONSHOT EFFECT: DISRUPTING BUSINESS AS USUAL

Published by

WYNNEFIELD BUSINESS PRESS

Editors: Laurie Gibson, Lisa Wolff, and Steve Almond

Cover design and creative direction: Jenn White Topliff

Book design: Charles McStravick

ISBN: 978-0-9729643-1-9
Ebook ISBN: 978-0-9729643-2-6

PRINTED IN THE UNITED STATES OF AMERICA

CONTENTS

PREFACE

One day I was driving to have breakfast with my business partner Lisa. Lisa is habitually punctual—almost to a fault. So when she texted to say she was going to be five minutes late, it got my attention.

By the time I reached the parking lot, though, I was grateful for the few extra minutes because of a fascinating segment on National Public Radio about the Apollo 11 space program. The segment focused on President John Kennedy's decision to send a man to the moon and return him safely to Earth. The mission was issued as a challenge. If the United States could be first to send a man to the moon, Kennedy felt it would re-establish America's superiority over the Soviet Union during the Cold War.

Kennedy exercised extraordinary leadership, and his approach brilliantly conflated his Presidential persona with the courageous and daring astronauts.

As the segment ended I jumped from my car, worried that I'd left Lisa waiting. But instead, she, too, was getting out of her car. We laughed—Lisa was listening to the same Apollo 11 segment I was and, like me, didn't want to miss a single word.

We put aside our plan to prepare for an upcoming board meeting to talk instead about the Kennedy Moonshot. We discussed the impact of the moonshot on the country and on our own lives. We deconstructed what made the Apollo space initiative and President Kennedy's leadership so effective and compelling. We realized that Kennedy's challenge to go where no human had gone before was not just about going to the moon; it was about harnessing human aspiration to accomplish something extraordinary, something that seemed nearly impossible to achieve.

The Moonshot.

We discussed the implications and drew parallels to our experiences in business, because that's what we do. We work with executives to achieve greater impact and inspire excellence in the people who make up the heart of their business.

We defined a moonshot as a complex, large-scale objective that can be accomplished only when teams abandon "business as usual."

Moonshots require significant breakthroughs in attitude, innovation, leadership, processes, management, and technology. They demand extraordinary execution and are often marked by seemingly unrealistic time lines.

Most moonshots are driven by a desire to be the first, or the best, or the fastest. They disrupt the status quo.

Lisa and I counted the business moonshots we had been involved with—individually and together. Eighteen. This number blew us away. Most people, if they are lucky, get to participate in one or two during their careers. It seems that Lisa and I have a knack for instigating impossible projects.

My first real moonshot was in the 1990s with the creation of the PalmPilot—the precursor to the smartphone. Lisa's most memorable moonshot was Nokia's MOSH, the first big mobile social sharing platform, which swelled to 13 million users in its debut year. It was our realization of our extensive experience with moonshots that planted the seeds for this book.

Later, as we interviewed colleagues and clients who had led and taken part in moonshots, we discovered something unexpected.

Most of the people we interviewed had forgotten a whole host of business impacts they had created via the moonshot. They had forgotten that their moonshot resulted in making the Inc. list of most innovative companies, and the millions of dollars of revenue they generated. They had forgotten about shareholder value, return on investment, and profit margins.

Instead, they remembered the near-miracles they accomplished through the sheer force of teamwork, determination, and dogged execution. They told us about careers that had been catapulted into the stratosphere. They reminded us of the everyday employees who had become superstars by making heroic contributions. They revealed the behind-the-scenes camaraderie, passion, and pride people felt because they were involved in something remarkable.

The interviews led us to a fundamental conclusion about moonshots: while they create extraordinary business impact, the magic of a moonshot is the profound impact on the people who create them. Moonshots are an act of human courage, imagination, and determination—writ large. When a business summons those qualities in its people, both the employees and the company are transformed.

Moonshots elevate contribution and challenge people to perform beyond what they think possible. In Lisa's work alone, more than half of the executives who ran the moonshot projects were promoted to CEO within two years. Moonshots also create strong bonds of loyalty and friendship. Lisa and I are proof of that.

Our hope in writing this book is that we will inspire you to summon the courage and resources to champion and participate in a moonshot. Because each time you are involved in a moonshot, you harness the best of your energies and skills, and experience the exhilaration that comes when you escape business as usual.

LISA GOLDMAN & KATE PURMAL

INTRODUCTION

When John F. Kennedy took office as the 35th president of the United States in 1961, America was locked in geopolitical crisis. Communism was taking hold in North Korea. In Cuba, Castro's alliance with the Soviet Union brought the potential for Soviet missiles closer to home. With the launch of the Sputnik satellite in 1957, the Soviets claimed an early lead in the space race as a Communist triumph.

Missiles were the measure of military might in the Atomic Age, and airspace the unclaimed military frontier. The nuclear threat was deeply ingrained in the American psyche, as schoolchildren practiced crouching under their desks in case of missile attacks. The threat was real.

In the first months of his presidency, Kennedy searched for a national achievement that would establish America's superiority. He asked National Aeronautics and Space Administration (NASA) advisors to identify a space program that would deliver dramatic results, and that the United States could win. NASA counseled Kennedy that to achieve supremacy, they had to search beyond what was already possible. The Soviet Union could not

ace of the moon with existing rocket technology; this gave
ates the best chance of taking the lead.

on has always exerted a powerful pull on the human imagination. But in 1961, when rockets routinely crashed on launch, and leaving Earth's orbit was still in the future, the moon seemed more distant than ever. By choosing to land people on the moon, Kennedy connected centuries of imagination with the world of technology and business. He changed the story line from military one-upmanship to human aspiration.

In May 1961, President Kennedy issued his bold challenge to Congress and the nation to land a man on the moon by the end of the decade.

> 66 I believe that this nation should commit itself
> to achieving the goal, before this decade is out,
> of landing a man on the moon and returning
> him safely to Earth. 99
>
> JOHN F. KENNEDY,
> speech to Congress, May 1961

Kennedy was convinced that with a strong national commitment, the United States could be the first country to land on the moon. His challenge appealed to America's spirit of adventure and patriotism. America responded; the mission to the moon mobilized the efforts of more than 400,000 people in business, universities, and government throughout the decade. Teams from companies including Boeing, North American Aviation, McDonnell Douglas, and the Grumman Corporation built six individual spacecrafts. Each mission required roughly five-and-a-half million parts manufactured by a host of subcontractors.

We know how this momentous story ends. On July 20, 1969, at 10:56 p.m. Eastern Daylight Time, Neil Armstrong climbed down the lunar module ladder and took the first steps on the surface of the moon, proclaiming, "That's one small step for a man, one giant leap for mankind."

But there is more to the story, because the first moon landing left its mark well beyond the lunar surface.

RIPPLE EFFECTS FROM THE MOONSHOT

The Apollo 11 mission achieved its goal of sending a man to the moon and back only five months shy of Kennedy's ambitious deadline. The United States scored a huge victory in the Cold War by demonstrating supremacy in the space race and proving that American innovation could achieve the unimaginable.

As one might expect, the Moonshot fueled scientific discoveries and inventions that spread to the broader economy. The original Moonshot set in motion a series of scientific and engineering innovations that have altered the landscape of the world in which we live. The technological legacy of the lunar missions is embedded in products as varied as running shoes, solar panels, pacemakers, and battery-powered tools.

But the long-term effects also played out in unexpected ways.

The quest for the moon advanced business practices on Earth. NASA coordinated the efforts of thousands of agency staff, outside contractors, and research universities. In managing this complex project, the agency established a fully integrated management and leadership structure for the various elements of the program. Leaders developed project-management techniques, including distributed decision-making authority and contingency planning. Many of these practices were integrated into the business world and remain instrumental to our economic engine today.

Born from a military crisis, the moon landing united people across nations. More than half a billion people, or about one-fifth of the world's population at the time, gathered around televisions to watch the historic event. Images transmitted from space changed perceptions of our role on Earth and the edges of human possibility, and gave us a different perspective of being citizens of one planet.

The lunar missions launched a generation of leaders and heroes. The Moonshot demonstrated that when people work together in service of an inspiring objective, nearly anything is possible. The moon landing was not the work of a few super scientists or NASA geniuses. It happened because thousands of people contributed tirelessly toward a single, improbable goal.

President Kennedy's speech at Rice University in September 1962 foreshadowed the significant human effects of the lunar mission:

> 66 We choose to go to the Moon in this decade
> and do the other things, not because they
> are easy, but because they are hard,
> because that goal will serve to organize
> and measure the best of our energies and skills,
> because that challenge is one that we are
> willing to accept, one we are unwilling
> to postpone, and one which we
> intend to win. 99

JOHN F. KENNEDY,
speech at Rice University, September 1962

We set our sights on the moon to elevate ourselves.

The story of the Moonshot serves as both inspiration and guide for anyone who aspires to extraordinary leadership or meaningful work with others. It demonstrates what can happen when you marry visionary leadership with human aspirations. History teaches us that launching a moonshot ignites innovation and brings forth the best in people, teams, and organizations.

A MOONSHOT TODAY

Many of today's business leaders weren't yet born when man first set foot on the lunar surface. But the Moonshot is still relevant in the twenty-first century. The original Moonshot (with a capital M) presents a compelling and inspiring lesson in how to achieve the remarkable.

A recent resurgence of the term *moonshot* by Google and others in the technology industry alludes to the original event, using the word to refer to any barely possible objective. But we're going to be more precise.

In this book, a moonshot is a compelling and worthy objective that's hard to achieve, because:

- It requires significant scientific or technological breakthroughs

- It demands that organizations and teams change how they operate

- It operates within a compressed time frame

You don't have to go to the moon to experience the moonshot effect.

Moonshots can encompass a specific project or drive the entire company.

Every startup is a moonshot. Entrepreneurs start businesses to pursue new ideas and disrupt industries, searching for breakthroughs in technology and business processes. Without an established business-as-usual culture, teams forge their own ways of working together. Startups execute quickly, with limited time and funding.

In mature companies, successful moonshots are often treated like a startup within the larger business. They are given tight timelines, with limited, milestone-based funding. Advisors and sponsors function as a board of directors. Leaders insulate teams from the bureaucratic gravity of the larger organization. Teams develop their own way of working, often distinct from the broader corporate culture. Operating within this separate environment, teams can identify and produce breakthroughs that would have been unthinkable in the typical business culture.

A moonshot isn't defined by its distance from Earth, but by its distance from business as usual.

The real value of the moonshot isn't achieving the stated objective, but the remarkable transformations in the people that endeavor to make the moonshot happen—*the moonshot effect*. The moonshot effect begins the moment you undertake the effort.

The human impact often transcends the business impact of the moonshot.

WHY THE MOON

Today's business leaders have inherited generations of discoveries and advances in science, technology, and human organization. To paraphrase Sir Isaac Newton, we stand on the shoulders of the giants. We have the opportunity and obligation to use the lessons of those who precede us to lead people and organizations in worthy pursuits.

We also live in a time of unprecedented innovation. The wonders of the near future sound like early science fiction stories: self-driving cars, purchases delivered by drones, and technology that tracks our every movement through the growing Internet of Things. Businesses must learn from the past while adapting to constant change.

Even when faced with overwhelming change, day in and day out we fall prey to the enormous gravitational pull of business as usual. Despite the best intentions, business leaders spend the majority of their time focusing on tactical issues, delivering short-term results to investors, and managing daily fire drills rather than shaping strategy and defining the future. We are figuratively crouching under our desks and hoping for the best, in the modern-day, business equivalent of the Cold War era's duck-and-cover drills.

Everyone hopes to join and lead agile, forward-thinking organizations that build lasting value through innovation. Remaining mired in the day-to-day prevents us from forging new paths.

If your business is stagnant, if you're facing a crisis, or if you're searching for a breakthrough to reach the next level of performance, consider launching a moonshot.

A moonshot is the antidote to the gravitational pull of day-to-day burdens. It requires people to discard their business-as-usual habits, and unites them in a collective endeavor to achieve something extraordinary. In the process, the teams and leaders who set out on the mission are transformed through the moonshot effect.

MISSION GUIDELINES

It's easy to talk about setting bold objectives as moonshots, but much harder to achieve them. If you are looking for a quick win or a magic bullet, put this book aside now.

Moonshots succeed only when leaders and teams break through the inertia of everyday operations. These efforts reveal problems and breakdowns; they also threaten the status quo. They put you in conflict with those who are content to work hard and make incremental progress. You *will* face resistance.

However, you will also start to experience the effects of the moonshot immediately, within yourself and those around you. The effect occurs in two primary spheres:

1. **MOONSHOTS TRANSFORM TEAMS.** Working together through the inevitable breakdowns makes teams stronger and more effective. In uniting people around a shared purpose, moonshots define a path to higher performance.

2. **MOONSHOTS LAUNCH HEROES AND LEADERS.** Working on a shared vision elevates the performance of individuals, tests and strengthens leadership effectiveness, and develops heroes from among the ranks.

The first section of this book guides you in identifying and implementing a moonshot. We'll dig deeper into what differentiates a moonshot from other objectives, while using a number of examples as templates. The second section describes the leadership skills that increase the odds of a successful landing. Part three offers practices for high-performing teams, to magnify the potential transformative effect on teams engaging in a moonshot. And part four offers practices and guidance for entrepreneurs piloting their own moonshot in the form of a startup.

If you're eager to elevate your leadership and cultivate the best in the people around you, it's time to launch a moonshot.

PART ONE

Moonshots

Ready to undertake a moonshot? In the chapters that follow, we will deconstruct the Kennedy Moonshot to extract what we can replicate and apply to moonshots in business. We'll use examples from the moonshots we have been involved with to demonstrate how they impact business, elevate leaders, and create high-performing people and teams.

You may identify and articulate your moonshot yourself, inspiring others around you to share your vision as President Kennedy did. Or your role may be to empower your team to generate ideas and find a compelling moonshot for your organization.

Whether you initiate the moonshot directly or provide support and urgency for others to set the course, the seven chapters in this section offer essential guidance. They are:

- **FROM THE MOON TO EARTH:** Applying the magic of the moon in business

- **THE ESSENTIAL INGREDIENTS OF A MOONSHOT:** How high the moon?

- **CHOOSE YOUR MOON:** Set the target for your moonshot

- **LIFTOFF:** Break free of business as usual

- **EXPECT THE UNEXPECTED:** The moonshot effect

- **MOONSHOTS AND STARTUPS:** Entrepreneurs who shoot for the moon

- **THE LAUNCH PLAN:** Seven steps to a moonshot

FROM THE MOON TO EARTH

The Magic of the Moon in Business

A moonshot taps into human aspirations to achieve something unexpected, difficult, and worthwhile.

There's no better template to leadership and organizational impact of a moonshot than John F. Kennedy and the Apollo 11 mission. But the book you're reading right now is about *business*, so we will also consider two well-known examples in industry: Alcoa in the 1980s and 1990s, under the leadership of CEO Paul O'Neill, and GE's Ecomagination initiative, instigated by CEO Jeff Immelt. They share characteristics that differentiate them from ordinary, aggressive business goals and instead catapult them to the level of a moonshot.

In the chapters that follow, we will dig into these stories, the qualities that link them, and what we can learn from them.

TO THE MOON AND BACK IN THE DECADE

In May of 1961, in the opening months of his presidency, President John F. Kennedy stood before Congress and the American people. In a speech titled "Urgent National Needs," he surprised Congress and the nation with his bold challenge to send a man to the moon and back before the end of the decade.

> **66** I believe that this nation should commit itself to achieving the goal, before this decade is out, of landing a man on the moon and returning him safely to Earth. **99**
>
> JOHN F. KENNEDY,
> speech to Congress, May 1961

As the original Moonshot that coined the term, you cannot get much bigger than this.

The objective surprised nearly everyone—especially those who understood what this challenge would truly entail. It was ambitious, unexpected, and galvanizing. The mission required the dedicated, coordinated efforts of hundreds of thousands of engineers and scientists and a budget more than $20 billion. Technologically, the experts were not certain the goal was possible, particularly within the constrained time frame.

As we will see in the chapters that follow, the Moonshot faced constant opposition and challenges. For the president, the stakes were high.

The speech took place one month after the Soviet Union sent the first man into space. America lagged its Cold War adversary in the space race, which was part of the escalating arms race between the countries. As mentioned earlier, Kennedy wanted to demonstrate America's leadership on the international stage. Reaching the moon first would be a clear win. The objective was as much political and cultural as technological.

The Apollo 11 mission met Kennedy's deadline by mere months. At the end of a tumultuous decade in the United States, the moon landing restored a collective national confidence. Although he did not live to see its fulfillment, Kennedy's legacy and leadership will be forever intertwined with the moon.

The story of the Moonshot continues decades after the astronauts' return to Earth. The effort instigated a series of scientific and engineering innovations, yet the greatest effect of the lunar mission may have been proving that when people work together in service of an aspirational and worthwhile objective, they rise to new levels of performance.

ALCOA SHOOTS FOR PERFECTION

Imagine for a moment that it is 1987, and you're an investor in Alcoa, the aluminum-manufacturing giant. You sit in an investors meeting, waiting to hear the latest CEO's plans for the company. Alcoa has faltered recently with failed product lines. You're hoping that the new guy, Paul O'Neill, has a plan to increase revenues and improve profitability.

Instead, O'Neill talks about worker safety, saying, "Every year, numerous Alcoa workers are injured so badly that they miss a day of work. Our safety record is better than the general American workforce, especially considering that our employees work with metals that are 1500 degrees and machines that can rip a man's arm off. But it's not good enough. I intend to make Alcoa the safest company in America. I intend to go for zero injuries."

Processing aluminum is hazardous; injuries were considered a regrettable but expected cost of doing business in the manufacturing industry. Alcoa at the time ranked in the top third of American companies for the fewest days lost to injury. Safety was an unlikely focus for the newly appointed CEO, given other issues facing the company, such as rising costs, labor unions, and market expansion.

But the enormous human toll of injuries became the focus for O'Neill's moonshot. The company gave the initiative the label "Zero is Possible," and it is still in place today. An example of the practices the company has installed to prevent life-threatening injury is their forklift safety policy. To avoid forklift-related injuries, employees must be in direct communications with the forklift operator before they are within three feet of their approach. Pedestrians in areas with high forklift traffic are required to wear safety vests.

Focusing intently and exclusively on worker safety turned out to be transformative. Alcoa's safety record became the industry ideal. During O'Neill's tenure at the company, injury rates at Alcoa dropped from

19 lost days per 1000 workers to less than two days—almost a tenfold decrease.

"Zero is Possible" was also good for business. In 2007, when O'Neill left to become U.S. Treasury Secretary, Alcoa's annual net income had grown five fold and its market capitalization had increased by $27 billion.

Clearly, many factors contributed to the company's financial performance during O'Neill's tenure. The safety initiative unlocked communications and innovation in ways that benefitted performance. But the core objective was about people, not profits. No matter the cause, the focus on safety did not hurt business performance. O'Neill proved the naysayers wrong.

GENERAL ELECTRIC'S ECOMAGINATION

In 2005, General Electric CEO Jeff Immelt announced that he was shifting the company to producing energy-efficient, ecologically friendly products, starting with a major investment in a program called "Ecomagination." At the time, GE was not a likely candidate to focus a program on developing environmentally efficient products. At the time, the company was widely believed to be one of the largest corporate polluters in the United States. Skeptical observers dismissed Immelt's announcement as a PR ploy designed to greenwash the company's poor environmental record. As with Paul O'Neill's announcement about worker safety at Alcoa, the initial reaction was one of surprise and disbelief.

Ten years later, the initiative has turned out to be a remarkably successful reinvention of GE. The company expects corporate purchases of eco-friendly machinery to drive significant growth by 2020, with fuel cell installations growing by 400 percent. It anticipates a fourfold increase in sales of LED lighting. Immelt's program has positioned the company with a significant business advantage.

A true commitment to the "Ecomagination" moonshot required GE to reengineer its entire product line for energy efficiency, including clothes dryers, lightbulbs, and jet engines. When Immelt called on Lorraine Bolsinger, Chief Marketing Officer for GE Aviation at the time, to run the program in 2005, products within the Ecosystems category accounted for

$10 million in revenue. Bolsinger and Immelt established the following clear, urgent targets:

- Double GE's $700 million research and development (R&D) investment in clean technology by 2010

- Turn a projected 40 percent increase in greenhouse gas emissions to a 1 percent reduction by 2012

- Cut its own use of water by 20 percent by 2012

"Ecomagination" proved successful well beyond its initial targets. By 2010, GE had invested $5 billion in clean tech R&D. By 2015, the program had generated more than $200 billion in sales. GE beat its environmental targets by a wide margin; by 2015, the company had reduced greenhouse gas emissions by 31 percent and water usage by 42 percent.

WHAT THEY HAVE IN COMMON

At first glance, processing aluminum, reducing greenhouse gas emissions, and putting a man on the moon have little in common. But digging deeper reveals shared elements of the three initiatives that are fundamental to a moonshot.

All of the examples cited were extremely difficult. In 1961, we hadn't yet developed the technology capable of launching a spacecraft to the moon. In 1987, Alcoa didn't know how to make the inherently dangerous job of aluminum manufacturing safer. Similarly, GE had to completely reengineer its products, redesign entire product lines and factories, and collaborate with customers to make use of the company's energy-efficient products.

These objectives carried a great deal of risk for the leaders as well as the people tasked with executing them. The risks of sending men into space are obvious. John F. Kennedy was staking his legacy on his public pronouncement with a bold, barely possible deadline.

A true moonshot brings with it the possibility of failure. It's tempting to focus on a safe goal or an incremental gain that you are certain you can reach. But a genuine moonshot is a formidable undertaking that requires you to fundamentally change the way you do business.

Paul O'Neill similarly took a huge risk with his "Zero is Possible" objective. His goal alienated short-term investors. In the weeks following the speech in October 1987, the company's stock price plummeted from $56 per share to a low of $34 per share. In drawing attention to safety problems, O'Neill exposed the dark underbelly of the manufacturing industry. He highlighted the human suffering that manufacturing organizations everywhere wanted to downplay as a necessary cost of doing business.

People who lead moonshots must fight a strong current of doubt and detraction.

Early in O'Neill's tenure at Alcoa, a young man was killed on the job at a plant. O'Neill called all of the plant managers into a daylong meeting to examine the problems that led to the fatality. According to Charles Duhigg, author of *The Power of Habit*, O'Neill squarely took responsibility, and forced those around him to do the same. His statement was: "*We killed this man. It's my failure of leadership. I caused his death. And it's the failure of all of you in the chain of command.*"

O'Neill had the courage to speak publicly about a taboo topic, uncomfortable for everyone. He demanded that those in his ranks step up to an unprecedented level of collective responsibility. He could do this because the objective itself was about alleviating human suffering.

Beyond being risky and difficult, moonshots tap into something deeply human that convinces us that they are noble pursuits.

Immelt's moonshot put his credibility at significant risk, with skeptics inside and outside the company waiting to further dismiss the initiative as a failed effort to gloss over the company's past environmental sins. (GE and Immelt were targeted from both sides, with Fox News and the Green Party alike denouncing the "Ecomagination" effort as an empty marketing or an image campaign.) The new program forced GE to embrace transparency, releasing performance metrics. The initiative also required GE to reach beyond its boundaries, working with technology giant Intel to create smarter, more energy-efficient factories and with Walmart to distribute renewable products.

Finally, all three programs delivered an enduring moonshot effect, transforming the organizations and people involved. The teams involved in the Apollo 11 mission embodied a deep sense of pride for having participated in the success of a historic mission. The United States regained its national identity as a world leader and its faith that anything is possible. Alcoa experienced a drastic improvement in organizational performance.

Ecomagination transformed the technology culture within GE by integrating the company into the Silicon Valley ecosystem. The company's eco-friendly products include sensors that report a range of data, including equipment's fuel usage, speed, downtime, and efficiency. GE now develops software tools for optimizing efficiency of equipment and better managing power usage. Digitization allows GE to better serve its customers by deploying upgrades to systems through software.

Perhaps the most significant result of Ecomagination is the effect it has had on the supply chain. GE has proven that an investment in clean technology and greenhouse gas emission reduction can pay dividends, and has partnered with companies like Walmart that are following GE's lead to reduce emissions and leave a lighter environmental footprint.

The enduring legacy of the moonshot effect makes these difficult and risky challenges truly worthwhile.

Not every bold business objective carries the same magic. A moonshot is unexpected. It's hard. And it's worth it.

2

THE ESSENTIAL INGREDIENTS OF A MOONSHOT

How High the Moon?

C hoosing a nearly impossible objective and calling it a moonshot
isn't enough to make the magic happen.

Business objectives that have the power to inspire people, transform
organizations, and drive change share similar attributes, even across
diverse industries. A moonshot has three essential elements woven into
its very fabric:

- **IT'S UNEXPECTED:** Because it lives outside of business as
  usual, the moonshot is surprising.

- **IT'S HARD:** You cannot transform a business by doing
  more of what you're already doing. A moonshot demands
  breakthroughs and disruption.

- **IT'S WORTH IT:** Achieving a moonshot represents a major victory, tapping into the innate human aspiration to be the first or best at something.

A MOONSHOT IS UNEXPECTED

There was nothing ordinary or expected about putting a man on the moon in 1961. Even people who were familiar with the space program were surprised by the announcement. As Gene Kranz, Flight Director for the Apollo programs, describes the reaction to President Kennedy's announcement in his book *Failure Is Not an Option*:

> *To those of us who had watched our rockets keel over, spin out of control, or blow up, the idea of putting a man on the moon seemed almost too breathtakingly ambitious . . . Word about the speech spread like wildfire through our offices at Langley; all work eventually came to a halt and people began to offer various opinions. Most wondered if it was for real.*

Similarly, Paul O'Neill startled investors and employees alike when he challenged Alcoa to become the safest company in America. People expected him, in his speech to investors, to focus on the usual topics like operating costs and revenues. One broker ran for a phone to warn investors to sell stock ahead of the anticipated rush. And when Jeff Immelt proposed "Ecomagination" to the top leaders of GE in December 2004, they voted him down.

A MOONSHOT IS HARD

66 It always seems impossible until it's done. **99**
NELSON MANDELA

Moonshots demand breakthroughs that are not possible within business-as-usual practices. They require individuals to stretch outside their comfort zones. Adhering to current ways of working can yield only incremental improvements. A moonshot requires and spurs disruption.

There's a fine line between plausible and impossible, and moonshots test that boundary. Some might call these bold ideas and efforts unreasonable. People will push back with plausible excuses for not stepping up to the challenge: *it's too difficult, it's not necessary, that's not how we do things*.

Yet moonshots demand that we defy those reasons.

66 There weren't very many of us who thought Apollo was reasonable the day that Mr. Kennedy said we were going to do it. We didn't even have a man in orbit yet. **99**

DR. CHRISTOPHER KRAFT,
first Flight Director at NASA

Alcoa's pursuit of a perfect safety record likewise seemed unreasonable to people in the manufacturing industry. O'Neill knew that to inspire breakthroughs, he first had to engineer a major and unexpected breakdown. And GE's transformation and change of focus to its environmental impact required enormous shifts in products and culture alike.

A MOONSHOT IS WORTH IT

People in organizations are hungry for leaders who challenge them to do meaningful and inspiring work. A moonshot taps into deep human aspirations. Nothing inspires camaraderie or teamwork more effectively than a collective desire to win, or to be best or first in something, or to achieve something truly meaningful.

Kennedy referred to his challenge to send a man to the moon and bring him back as an objective "which we intend to win." Paul O'Neill, too, set his sights high. He didn't aim to just "improve" worker safety. Instead, he told investors, "I intend to make Alcoa *the safest company in America*." The entire company aspired to perfection, with no safety incidents.

Perfection may ultimately be impossible, but pursuing it makes many unexpected things possible.

In your own business, finding a moonshot may require creativity. If being number one in your industry is unrealistically ambitious, consider achieving leadership in a specific segment or vertical market. Look for an objective with a human pull, a goal worth rallying around and pursuing.

Finding Your Moonshot Using Three Questions

As you search for ideas, ask the following:

1. **WHAT WILL SURPRISE PEOPLE?** If people expect it, it's not a moonshot. Can you come up with a bold objective that's unexpected or surprising?

2. **WHAT WILL CAUSE US TO BREAK NEW GROUND?** A moonshot challenges the status quo and requires people to abandon or question established practices.

3. **WHAT CAN WE BE FIRST OR BEST AT?** What will get people fired up? A moonshot should inspire excellence. Can you be best in the world at something? Can you get there first? Is the goal something that people are excited about pursuing?

OHASHI'S TRIATHLON

Zen Ohashi is the CEO of a management consulting firm in Japan. While working with Lisa, he sought a moonshot that would strengthen the connections between his independent consultants.

IT'S UNEXPECTED: Ohashi challenged the entire team of 25 consultants to train for and finish the Hawaii Triathlon, less than a year away. The scope of the athletic endeavor, and the tight time frame alike, surprised the team.

IT'S HARD: In Japanese culture, people tend to agree with the CEO's directives. Ohashi's team was no exception. However, it quickly became apparent that the challenge was more formidable than Ohashi had initially imagined. Several of the consultants did not know how to swim, most didn't own a bike, and only a few had ever run a race.

Several of the consultants came to Ohashi and said, "If we leave everyone to train on their own, we're setting ourselves up for failure." They proposed pooling their resources to hire the best coaches in Japan to support their team's training efforts. This changed everything. These coaches had trained Olympic triathletes and established rigorous training programs for Ohashi's team.

IT'S WORTH IT: Less than a year later, all 25 people started and finished the race. More surprisingly, the excitement of their effort recruited others to join; the team almost doubled in size. Six team members' wives participated, and several children finished the kids' triathlon. Three of the firm's clients and seven family members created their own teams and joined the race, as well. Lisa and her husband, Howard, also completed the triathlon. What started as an internal team-building moonshot expanded to enhance the team's relationships with families and clients.

The excitement of pursuing a moonshot pulls in others around you, expanding its impact.

The most surprising side effect was the effect it had on the consultants' collective business. At the outset, team members worried that time spent training would hamper their ability to sustain revenue. Instead, revenues grew during the training. The consultants strengthened client relationships and generated a renewal pipeline for the following year.

CHOOSE
YOUR MOON

Set the Target for Your Moonshot

Now that you know what a moonshot looks like and how it differs from ordinary business, it's time to answer the important question: How do you find a moonshot for your business?

Everyone loves stories about people who are struck with inspiration in an "Aha!" moment, like the apple hitting Newton on the head. In reality, however, breakthrough ideas rarely appear out of nowhere.

President Kennedy conferred with NASA's engineers before the May 1961 address to Congress. He asked the experts whether the United States had a chance of beating the Soviets in a major space milestone, such as putting a laboratory into orbit, making a trip around the moon, or landing on the moon. He actively searched for an objective that would propel the United States into global leadership in the space race. He landed on the idea that had the most resonance and impact.

Leaders often believe it's their job to come up with big ideas. Consider instead that your role as a leader may be to challenge and inspire *others* to find a moonshot.

WHAT'S THE BIG IDEA?

Lee Epting was a vice president at Nokia in 2006, before the arrival of the Apple iPhone, when Nokia held a dominant position in the cell phone market. In a span of a little over six months, her team launched a groundbreaking social networking platform for sharing photos, games, music, and other content on mobile devices. When it launched in 2007, the Nokia MOSH platform quickly ramped up to 13 million users. And it earned the company a place on *Inc.* magazine's 25 Top Most Innovative Companies list.

The project began with a challenge from another company vice president, recently appointed to Lee's area. After a meeting in which she presented her team's current projects and status, he confronted her with this question: "But what's the big idea?"

Epting realized that she didn't have one. She left the meeting in shocked silence, and with an implicit mandate to find a breakthrough idea. She met with Lisa to debrief from the meeting, and they agreed the situation warranted immediate action. Epting picked up the phone and called five star employees—including people not on her team—and told them to drop everything and come to her office for an emergency meeting.

She selected individuals with creative, operational, engineering, system architecture, and sales backgrounds. Says Epting, "I thought of it like baking a cake; you had to have all the right ingredients."

Within two minutes, everyone had assembled in her office, bracing to hear about an emergency. She said, "Our business needs a *big idea*. And I'm challenging you to be the team that finds it." She told them she intended to clear their schedules so they could work exclusively on this project. Then she defined the requirements:

- **BUSINESS IMPACT:** The proposed project should have a significant business impact, with aggressive growth targets. In other words, it had to be a major win for Nokia.

- **TIMELINE:** The team had 45 days to produce a business plan for the idea. Once the plan was approved, they had to deliver the idea to market within six months.

- **VISIBILITY:** The idea should be unexpected and visible throughout the company and the broader market.

She instructed the team, "Don't even go back to your offices except to get your stuff. It's my job to clear your schedules, and I'm going to meet with your managers now." The disruption of daily business started at that moment.

She then asked them to choose an offsite location where they could work, and to come back in a week with one or more ideas that met her requirements. With no limitations on the location, she fully expected the team to head to Hawaii, Bali, or some other exotic location to find creative inspiration.

Instead, they chose to convene in an isolated cabin in the woods in Finland. The lodging there gives the word "rustic" a bad name. The team slept in dormitory-style rooms with narrow cots, worn woolen blankets, scratchy towels, and a single tiny bar of soap per person.

Even more surprising—and especially for employees of a smartphone leader—the cabin had *no electricity*. It was about as far from the business-as-usual environment that the team could get.

After a week, they presented initial concepts to Lee. These included "Trusted Voice," a set of pre-selected content; "MyCatalogs," a mobile shopping experience; and "Widget Service," a curated selection of mini-applications. The concept they chose with was Nokia MOSH: a software platform for sharing content on mobile phones.

The idea met the three requirements of a moonshot:

- **IT'S UNEXPECTED:** Nokia was at heart a hardware company; no one expected it to deliver a content-sharing platform. More surprising to the Nokia executives, the platform would work across all mobile phones, not just Nokia models.

- **IT'S HARD:** The project encountered internal barriers and resistance. Epting's team was not a product-development group. The company had to pioneer not only technological but also legal solutions, such as how to manage liability related to user-posted content on its networks. According to Epting, "We were stepping over boundaries and pushing limits."

- **IT'S WORTH IT:** The idea of a social network that worked across various types of phones delivered a major market coup for Nokia at the time. And the individuals who took part were forever changed.

While Epting's moonshot did not ultimately prevent Nokia's later decline in the mobile phone market, it did transform the people and organizations involved in a way that left a lasting and unexpected impact.

The effort tested Lee's leadership skills. She didn't come up with the specifics of the moonshot; her team did that. Her role was to assemble the right team, set the guidelines, and then create an environment in which her team could succeed. She had to step back and let the team be the heroes. "As a leader," she said, "you often feel like you have to do the heavy lifting. I watched my team do the heavy lifting. I had to come up with new ways to support them, clearing runways without them knowing it, and creating white space for them to operate in. I also had to shield them from the resistance you find in a large company—naysayers and people wanting to block the project."

Moonshots develop new generations of leaders and heroes.

The moonshot also developed another generation of leaders and heroes. The team members went on to successful careers, and launched moonshots in their next roles and companies. Moonshots are contagious.

It all started with that simple challenge: What's the big idea?

LIFTOFF

Break Free of Business as Usual

A spacecraft must achieve a speed of 7 miles per second, or nearly 25,000 miles per hour, to break free of Earth's gravity without falling back to the surface or returning to orbit. That's the *escape velocity* for our planet.

Innovative ideas likewise must achieve escape velocity from the gravity of business as usual. Once you've found your moonshot, improve your odds of achieving escape velocity by making it public and standing firm.

MAKE IT PUBLIC

President Kennedy could have submitted a request for NASA-related funding through the usual channels. Instead, he used the occasion of a speech to the U.S. Congress on the subject of Urgent National Needs to declare his objective of reaching the moon. He chose the most public forum available.

Make your moonshot public. Announce it in a high-profile venue, such as in front of the board or at an all-hands meeting. The public forum calls on people to take a stand. If handled well, it increases commitment and the likelihood that the moonshot will happen.

Making your moonshot public builds momentum and commitment.

Before you take your moonshot out into the world, package it to make the commitment both clear and compelling. The following ideas can help to increase your chances of success.

- **DITCH THE JARGON.** Even though it was rocket science, everyone from NASA engineers to average citizens could understand the concept of landing a man on the moon and bringing him home.

- **MAKE IT HUMAN.** The most powerful and inspirational ideas speak to a human need or desire. Kennedy connected his Moonshot in human terms: putting a man on the moon and bringing him safely home. People could look up into the night sky and envision what it might be like to step onto that distant moon.

- **START THE CLOCK.** Without a deadline, a moonshot is just a dream. Kennedy's declared timeline of the end of the decade seemed far too short for those who understood the magnitude of the challenge.

A compressed deadline can turn a bold objective into a moonshot.

STAND FIRM

Resistance to a moonshot often comes from the people who best understand the challenges involved. They object to the simplicity of the moonshot because it masks underlying complexity.

However, a moonshot is an ideal structure with which to tackle complexity. Moonshots have a way of revealing and resolving issues that live far outside their core objectives.

Although most businesses are driven by revenue and profit, a moonshot doesn't need a financial target to have a significant economic impact. Alcoa's "Zero is Possible" objective was *not* to reduce the cost of days due to injury. The goal was to make employees safer.

A simple, non-financial objective can cut through complexities that ultimately affect revenue and profit.

Simplicity is powerful in a complex world.

Many highly intelligent people build careers by figuring out how to mitigate complexity. From Silicon Valley technology companies to universities and beyond, mastering complexity is a valued skill. The highly intelligent masters of complexity may voice objections wrapped in phrases like:

"We tried that already."

"You're not taking into account ..."

"That makes sense except for ..."

The best way to resolve these types of concerns is to focus the discussion on the future: "Assuming that we can solve these problems, is this a goal worth pursuing?" Acknowledge the interrelatedness of the objective and the objections: "Is it possible that in the course of achieving this goal, we'll uncover ways to approach other challenges we see today?"

When you shift your perspective from the current, business-as-usual reality to the future, you gain allies and galvanize support. Use the *pull* of your future vision to break through immediate obstacles and objections. If you can get those smart, detail-oriented people to glimpse the future you see, they may become your most valuable partners.

66 The man-in-space program was simple in concept, difficult in execution. Every mission was a first, a new chapter in the book. 99

GENE KRANZ,
Failure Is Not an Option

KENNEDY STANDS FIRM

Transcripts of presidential meetings reveal that John F. Kennedy had to fight for his Moonshot, even with the people who eventually made it happen. Here's part of a discussion with NASA Administrator James Webb and others about whether the lunar landing should be NASA's top objective, or whether the president should dial back the objective to American "preeminence in space," a more vague goal that would support other efforts in the agency.

> JAMES WEBB: All right, then let me say this. If I go out and say that this is the number-one priority and that everything else must give way to it, I'm going to lose an important element of support for your program and for your administration.
>
> PRESIDENT KENNEDY [interrupting]: By who? Who? What people? Who?
>
> JAMES WEBB: By a large number of people.
>
> PRESIDENT KENNEDY: Who? Who?
>
> JAMES WEBB: Well, particularly the brainy people in industry and in the universities . . .

After more discussion, the president made his decision to keep the lunar landing as the top priority, thanked the group, and left the room. Remember this when you're dealing with pushback from those who want less ambitious objectives.

Great leaders demonstrate an unfaltering commitment to their vision.

EXPECT THE UNEXPECTED

The Moonshot Effect

When selling the moonshot to others, it's tempting to focus solely on the direct benefits of achieving the objective. These might include increased market share, revenue growth, competitive advantage, or other compelling business benefits.

Don't confuse the business benefits with the greater effect. As previously mentioned, the moonshot effect extends beyond direct business benefits, and may have greater long-term value to the organization and individuals involved.

To paraphrase President Kennedy, we undertake a moonshot to organize and measure the best of our energies and skills. The act of doing so elevates and amplifies people's abilities, delivering profound change and wide-reaching impact.

The moonshot effect is the accumulation of far-reaching benefits that result from pursuing a difficult goal.

The moonshot effect often plays out in unexpected ways. You cannot explicitly plan for these effects, but you can actively look for them, and support and sustain them as they arise.

In our work with leaders who have launched moonshots, years later they talk almost exclusively about the moonshot effects. Lee Epting had actually forgotten that her MOSH project landed Nokia on *Inc.* magazine's Top 25 Most Innovative Companies list. What she remembered instead was the *human* impact. Nearly a decade later she was still deeply moved recalling the party she threw to celebrate the team's successful launch of MOSH, particularly the sense of pride and camaraderie that filled the room that day.

THE EFFECTS OF THE APOLLO MISSIONS

Historians are still analyzing and tallying the widespread effects of the original Moonshot: microcomputers, calls for democracy in the Soviet Union, insulation technologies, and high-speed data communications are just a few.

Beyond technology, in racing to the moon, we designed practices here on Earth to address the magnitude of the project. These practices are embedded in today's business environments and include project management techniques, distributed decision-making, and the use of simulations.

But the greatest effect of the lunar missions may have been cultural.

The manned Apollo missions offered the public a broader perspective of our own planet. Live television images of Earth from space, the famous Earth Rise photo from the Apollo 8 mission, and the iconic Blue Marble image of Earth taken during the Apollo 17 flight captured imaginations and fueled growing environmental awareness. The high-quality images generated by various space flights triggered interest in satellite Earth photography, which has itself influenced countless disciplines. By leaving Earth, we have come to understand it better.

The long tail of the lunar mission is long indeed, its ripple effect lasting for generations to come.

> *The effects of a moonshot, both big and small,*
> *become the stories that are remembered and retold.*

Capture and share these effects to serve as inspiration for yourself, your teams, and those who follow.

MOONSHOTS, TEAMS, AND ORGANIZATIONS

As we've said before, moonshots change people and teams that undertake them.

At Alcoa, the "Zero is Possible" concept has remained a consistent part of the company's corporate culture over multiple decades. Alcoa employees took advantage of new communication channels created for safety recommendations, opening floodgates for creative ideas that otherwise would never have reached the ears of management. One group in Rockdale, Texas, invented a smelting process. A team at a plant facing layoffs figured out how to reduce furnace downtime by 50 percent, saving Alcoa millions of dollars while preserving jobs. Another worker suggested reconfiguring the painting machines for aluminum siding so they could switch out pigments quickly to respond to customer demand. Within a year, profits on aluminum siding doubled.

To this day, the company publishes its current injury statistics on its website, and stands behind "Zero is Possible." This simple idea has sustained a lasting cultural transformation, and the company continues to make progress.

For Nokia, the direct market share boost from its moonshot was transitory. But the success of the project transformed the teams that undertook the effort. The initial five players, a disparate group, became a tightly knit team. People in the larger group expressed pride being associated with the MOSH initiative. Lee Epting says, "The project galvanized people in a way I could not have imagined."

THE PEOPLE OF THE MOON

Moonshots affect teams, individual contributors, and leaders on the mission.

A moonshot creates opportunities to identify and promote heroic actions among teams. It challenges people to venture beyond their comfort zones and gives them an opportunity to achieve something significant toward a shared purpose. The pursuit of a moonshot inspires creativity, courage, and collaboration—all valuable attributes in today's business environment.

> **66 Amazing how quickly you adapt— why, it doesn't seem weird at all to me to look out there and see the moon going by. 99**
>
> MICHAEL COLLINS, ASTRONAUT,
> FROM THE APOLLO 11 LOG

Leaders who pursue moonshots hone their visionary skills and elevate their leadership skills by becoming hero-makers.

Moonshots are addictive.

The key players on Lee Epting's team at Nokia have moved on to other jobs, but carry with them the experience of succeeding in a moonshot. Former team members still contact Epting when they engage in moonshots, and refer back to their experience at Nokia as a guidepost.

MOONSHOTS AND STARTUPS

Entrepreneurs Who Shoot for the Moon

The tech startup community loves to talk about moonshots, and for good reason. Every startup is a moonshot.

An entrepreneur is someone who takes on a moonshot without the safety net of an established organization. They are the captains who launch and pilot missions with small crews, limited fuel supplies, and short runways. They often fail, but emerge changed and transformed by the effort.

Serial entrepreneurs return time and again to the challenge of launching a startup. Why? Perhaps they are addicted to the potency of the startup moonshot effect.

THE STARTUP AS MOONSHOT

Startups exhibit the key attributes of a moonshot:

Startups are unexpected. Many startups are bent on disrupting the status quo. Entrepreneurs search for "big ideas" that represent surprising, game-changing innovations. Startups do things differently.

Startups are hard. Entrepreneurs, like rocket scientists, undertake difficult feats that require numerous breakthroughs. They are intensely focused on the burn rate of their fuel and time remaining to touchdown. Even with generous funding, startups have a limited time window to execute their plans. Compressed time frames add urgency. Everyone engaged in a startup accepts significant risk.

Startups are worthwhile. When they succeed, startups build businesses, employ people, create wealth, reshape industries, and transform careers. Even when they fail, the lessons learned are invaluable.

As with other moonshots, those who engage in startups experience a lasting effect.

At the highest levels, successful startup teams forge working relationships that often span companies and careers. Teams tend to re-form and work with each other, again and again. They support and inspire each other's future ventures. In part, it is because they have worked together to overcome significant challenges and achieve something extraordinary. They share an addiction to the rush of the moonshot. The so-called PayPal Mafia is a great example; this group of early employees from PayPal has gone on to reshape the technology industry, starting companies including Tesla, LinkedIn, YouTube, Yelp, and others. The shared setbacks and struggles faced in the early years of the company cemented relationships and experiences that contributed to their future successes.

The moonshot effect at a startup permeates well beyond the founding team. Throughout the organization, the people who work for fast-moving startups often find themselves attracted to the challenge and their ability to make an impact through their efforts.

THE MOONSHOT AS A STARTUP

Sometimes entrepreneurs don't set out to build a business. The business is the byproduct of pursuing the moonshot. This was, in part, the story of Lisa Kristine.

The accomplished humanitarian photographer Lisa Kristine has built her career documenting indigenous cultures in more than 100 countries on six continents. But she wanted to infuse her work with greater purpose.

After encountering the Free the Slaves organization, she set for herself the personal objective of using her photography to mobilize action against human slavery. She began to photograph the human face of slavery around the world, publishing her images in books and documentaries.

Lisa Kristine's own business has evolved through the effort. Today she is a sought-after speaker. Her TED talk, "Photos that bear witness of human slavery," has over two million views. In 2013, she won the Lucie Humanitarian Award, the photography industry's equivalent of an Academy award. She creates books and documentaries, and was the inspiration behind the character Sofia in the 2014 full feature film *SOLD,* produced by Oscar award–winning team Emma Thompson and Jeffrey Brown. In 2014, Lisa Kristine was invited to the Vatican to witness Pope Francis and 25 world religious leaders sign a declaration to end slavery by 2020. Her profession has grown around her commitment to ending human slavery.

This moonshot has had many unexpected ripple effects, for Lisa Kristine's own business and beyond.

An eight-year-old girl named Vivienne Harr saw one of Lisa Kristine's photos of children in slavery. She was inspired to set up a lemonade stand to support efforts to end slavery. That simple business has grown into Make a Stand, a B-corporation that donates a percentage of its profits to ending child slavery.

Businesses launch moonshots,
and moonshots launch businesses.

THE LAUNCH PLAN

Seven Steps to a Moonshot

If we have convinced you of the power of the moonshot effect, you may be wondering how to make it happen in your business or life.

Good news: Getting started is easy. You don't even have to read this entire book before you begin, although you'll want to refer to it along the way. You can launch a moonshot almost immediately, if you have determination and the right people.

Here's our favorite formula for putting the magic of a moonshot to work within an existing organization. It costs little to execute this launch plan through step five. At that point, you will know if the moonshot is worth the resources, time, and money necessary to get it off the ground.

STEP ONE: **CALL THE MOONSHOT MEETING**

Start by choosing a cross-functional team of six to eight people. In a large organization, reach beyond your own group or area of responsibility. Your goal is to build a team with diverse and complementary skill sets, perspectives, and expertise.

Choose individuals who are rock stars in their own areas. Find candidates who have as many of the following attributes as possible:

- Excellent communication and collaboration skills

- High degree of self-motivation

- Strong time management skills

- Willingness to take on challenges

- History of delivering on promises and meeting deadlines

- High energy

- Forward-thinking perspective

Having identified the team, call an emergency meeting. Using the term *emergency* implants urgency from the inception of the project. Mystery and intrigue play a role as well; the meeting, like the moonshot, is unexpected.

Send a short-notice invitation, or have an assistant or colleague pull the targeted people from whatever they're doing, with an urgent request: "Lisa has asked that you drop everything and come to her office in 15 minutes."

Once in the meeting, start by acknowledging *why* you have invited this particular group of people. Describe the traits or expertise that each person brings to the team. Then describe the concept of a moonshot in as much detail as possible, including the specific ways you see it helping the company, the industry, and customers (more on that below).

Invite them to be the core team on a moonshot. Make it clear that they are being offered the chance to participate in a venture that has a significant impact on the business. It will be highly visible and challenging—the kind of activity that reshapes careers.

Lay out the commitments to continue.

- Team members will commit time to the effort over the next 45 days, with the possibility of extending beyond that period if the project is approved. We recommend that team members commit at least 50 percent of their time for the first 45 days.

- As the moonshot champion, you commit to providing guidance and resources to ensure their success, to working with their managers to free their time, and to running interference while they undertake the initial phase of the moonshot.

Ask the team members to sign on with you. Moonshots require eager, willing participants.

We choose to go to the moon; the choice is not made for us.

STEP TWO: ISSUE THE CHALLENGE

Issue the challenge to the team: find a moonshot. You already know what a moonshot is—something that's difficult, unexpected, and worthwhile. But those qualities are intangible. Define clear, measurable criteria for the moonshot, using metrics relevant to your business. These may include:

- Revenue impact

- Customer or market share growth

- Industry visibility

- Being first to market

- Investment or budget guidelines

- Return on Investment (ROI) or break-even requirements

Give the team one week to come up with a list of five proposals that meet your criteria. Then send them somewhere to get started on the process.

The idea-generating process works best when it takes place at an off-site location, ideally over at least two or three days. Why? Because it's difficult to disrupt business as usual when you're sitting in the middle of it.

When you remove people from the day-to-day environment, they think more creatively and adopt different perspectives. Working intensely together as a group, outside of everyday roles, strengthens connections between team members.

STEP THREE: CHOOSE YOUR MOON

As mentioned above, at the end of the week, ask the team to present five proposals, along with their recommendations. Work together to select one idea, refining it as necessary. This will be your moonshot.

Now give the team the following mandate:

- Build a business case for the moonshot such that it will meet the business impact requirements you defined.

- Build the case on the assumption that, if approved, the team will have a specific timeline to implement. Short projects work best. Six months is ideal. Allot no more than 12 months to achieve a breakthrough milestone, such as shipping a product, launching a service, or making another significant change to business as usual.

- Be ready to present the business case for approval in 45 days.

- Present specific, credible evidence of product/market fit.

STEP FOUR: BUILD THE BUSINESS CASE

The team spends the next 45 days refining the proposal and creating the business case. In parallel, team members validate the idea with customers, industry experts, and other advisors. You are the executive champion for the moonshot. The moonshot may develop and come into sharper focus during this phase.

We recommend creating a dedicated physical space where the core team can work together on the project. Some teams move to a separate building or remote location. Others set up a dedicated "war room" where they meet regularly, and where their timelines, ideas, and concepts cover the walls. Separation from their day-to-day environments reinforces focus and commitment.

Up to this point, your investment in the moonshot is limited to the team's time. The downside risks are low, and the potential upside quite high. The validation process accelerates learning and innovation among the team members.

STEP FIVE: **SECURE COMMITMENT TO LAUNCH**

After 45 days, the moonshot team presents their plan to the people in the company who have the authority to approve it. The audience might be an executive team or board of directors. The presentation will include specific requests for funding and resources to execute the plan.

The first 45 days of the team's time commitment is now complete. As you request resources, include the team members' time to pursue the plan. If the project earns approval and funding, the clock starts ticking on the countdown to reach the moon.

STEP SIX: **EXECUTE THE PLAN**

Move into full execution mode.

Working backward from the launch date, have the team create a series of milestones that will get you to liftoff by the deadline you have identified. See the chapter "The Flight Path" in part three for details.

Because you're working on a tight deadline, schedule frequent, efficient check-ins. Frequency may vary depending on the phase of the project. When the team is tackling a tough issue, consider daily, rapid status checks. When things are going smoothly, schedule updates weekly or every other week.

We recommend that the team presents status updates to the executive champion every 30 days and a full project review every 90 days, so you can course-correct and secure additional funding or resources if needed.

As executive champion, you will work behind the scenes to assist them in breaking through bureaucratic obstacles and barriers to success, and to prevent day-to-day pressures from distracting members of the team.

STEP SEVEN: LAUNCH

The launch may be the opening salvo in something larger, a minimum viable product that demonstrates potential for greater impact. Either way, make sure the new product, program, or service makes a difference.

Having launched, honor the completion, both privately and publicly. Even if there's more work to do, celebrate the launch. The team has undertaken enormous effort to get to this point. To maintain momentum and reap the benefits of the moonshot effect, acknowledge and commend the efforts. See the chapter "Completions and Landings" in part three for thoughts on marking completion.

Make a big splash, in order to have the greatest impact on the team members and the organization as a whole. We recommend teams initiate both internal and external public relations efforts early on to garner support and enthusiasm and build momentum for the moonshot.

IT'S TIME TO GO

66 We said to ourselves that we have now done everything we know how to do. We feel comfortable with all of the unknowns that we went into this program with. We don't know what else to do to make this thing risk-free, so it's time to go. 99

DR. CHRISTOPHER C. KRAFT, JR.,
NASA Manned Spacecraft Center Director
of Flight Operations

The chapters that follow offer practices and suggestions for each phase of the launch plan; you have the necessary guidance at hand. Until you reach funding in step five, the costs of the launch plan are minimal: the team members' time and perhaps an off-site venue.

You could call that emergency meeting tomorrow. Or today. The barriers to starting are low.

What's your next moonshot? Initiate a launch plan and find out.

PART TWO

Bold Leadership

Pursuing a moonshot requires bold leadership, both within yourself and from those around you.

Boldness in this instance is a matter of impact, not attitude. It's about setting worthy objectives and developing the skills to achieve them. Bold leaders aren't brash and pushy—they are collaborative and empower others. Rather than being blind to risk, they are visionary about possibility. The most effective leaders act with confidence and exhibit humility.

A moonshot presents a unique opportunity to elevate leadership skills by uniting people behind a shared vision and objective. Effective leadership requires a focus on results rather than simply managing activity. Success depends on developing and nurturing the talents of the individual team members. The inevitable setbacks and breakdowns offer opportunities to hone leadership in tough situations.

Take advantage of the occasion of a moonshot to fine-tune your own leadership capacity and to identify and elevate the leaders and heroes around you. While these leadership practices apply in any business environment, we have found the ones outlined in the following chapters to be particularly important for anyone leading a moonshot:

- **ENVISION THE FUTURE:** The key to visionary leadership

- **SUIT UP:** Adopt stances that strengthen leadership

- **SECURE AN EXPLICIT COMMITMENT:** Get your mission approved

- **MAINTAIN THE SUPPLY LINES:** Connect consistently with CEOs, boards, and investors

- **THE POWER OF ACKNOWLEDGMENT:** Cultivate leadership by giving credit

- **ELEVATE YOUR PEOPLE SKILLS:** Small actions build and maintain rapport

- **EXPAND YOUR IMPACT:** Intentional networking

- **BE A HERO-MAKER, NOT A HERO:** Recognize and inspire heroic action

ENVISION THE FUTURE

The Key to Visionary Leadership

In September 1962, President Kennedy delivered a speech at Rice University in Houston, now known as the "We choose to go to the moon" speech. He shared the larger vision of the Moonshot with the Rice University community and the world at large, using powerful images and inspiring oratory:

> *We set sail on this new sea because there is a new knowledge to be gained, and new rights to be won, and they must be won and used for the progress of all people. . . . Whether it will become a force for good or ill depends on man, and only if the United States occupies a position of pre-eminence can we help decide whether this new ocean will be a sea of peace or a new terrifying theater of war . . . But why, some say, the Moon? Why choose this as our goal? And they may*

*well ask, why climb the highest mountain? Why—35 years
ago—why fly the Atlantic? . . . We choose to go to the Moon
in this decade and do the other things, not because they are
easy, but because they are hard, because that goal will serve
to organize and measure the best of our energies and skills,
because that challenge is one that we are willing to accept,
one we are unwilling to postpone, and one in which we
intend to win.*

The speech anchors the Moonshot in the context of historic human exploration: navigating the seas and skies, scaling mountain peaks. The president chose these images to resonate with the pioneering spirit of the American people, in an effort to gain continued support for the space program.

President Kennedy applied the practices of visionary leadership when he invited us to imagine a future reality together.

VISION IN BUSINESS

The revolutionary nature of a moonshot makes it the perfect vehicle for cultivating visionary leadership. A shared vision inspires teams and organizations to elevate their performance.

Vision plays a vital role for entrepreneurs or anyone pioneering a product category, an innovative device, or changed customer behavior. Visionary leaders steer teams toward unseen destinations as they develop and bring solutions to market.

Kate developed an appreciation for the power of visionary leadership as an early employee and member of the management team at Palm, Inc. Jeff Hawkins's, the founder, invented the concept for the PalmPilot before the smartphone and tablet of today. Like many innovators, Hawkins had a clear idea of what he wanted to create. He wanted his team to understand and share that personal vision as they developed the first PalmPilot, a handheld device unlike anything on the market at the time.

To make his vision come alive, he carved a balsa wood mock-up of his mental image of the PalmPilot and crafted the stylus from a bamboo chopstick. He carried this wooden prototype everywhere. He pulled it out during meetings, interacting with the block of wood much as customers would eventually use the real product.

Crazy? In Silicon Valley, startup entrepreneurs have permission to be a little crazy. But it was effective.

Hawkins' wooden prototype guided the engineering team through key product decisions. It inspired everyone in the company to navigate the challenges and roadblocks they faced in developing this breakthrough technology. Having a physical device clarified what was essential. The small screen area on the homemade prototype prevented the team from overburdening the design with extra features—the sin of "feature creep." It kept everyone focused on the ideal user experience.

This story illustrates two key points: the critical role of vision in leadership, and the magnetic pull of a strong vision—even when it's made of wood.

VISIONARY LEADERSHIP

Who would you rather work for: someone adept at navigating politics and climbing the corporate ladder, or someone who inspires people with a bold vision and sense of purpose? Most of us would rather work for a visionary leader.

As part of their ongoing research into leadership, authors James Kouzes and Barry Posner have surveyed tens of thousands of people around the world about the characteristics they look for in colleagues and leaders.

Honesty tops the list for both colleagues and leaders. But for leaders, *vision* ranks a close second. In contrast, only 27 percent look for vision in colleagues. Vision distinguishes leaders.

Visionary leadership is not exclusive to the upper ranks of management. People demonstrate vision by the way they lead projects or step up to take on challenges. Leadership can emerge organically at any level of the organization.

Perhaps you've taken the Myers-Briggs assessments. If so, chances are you didn't fall into one of the profiles associated with visionary leadership (INTJ and INFJ in Myers-Briggs terminology). According to the Myers-Briggs Foundation, these types represent 2.1 and 1.5 percent of the population, respectively.

A very small percentage of the population of the developed world fits the description of innate or natural visionaries. The rest of us don't think of ourselves as visionary.

What if we stop thinking of vision as an attribute that someone is born with, and instead realize that vision is a skill that we can cultivate and practice, like playing an instrument or swinging a golf club? From this perspective, visionary leaders are all around us, waiting to reveal their potential.

Visionary leadership is not an innate skill
you must be born with—vision can be learned.

You don't have to be one of those rare innate visionaries to use vision to your advantage. Everyone can imagine the future. But few of us behave like natural visionaries and step into the future to experience those visions.

WOMEN AND VISION

A study by Professor Herminia Ibarra of INSEAD (a business education organization) compared evaluations of more than 2,800 executives across 10 different leadership traits. For 9 of the 10 traits, women scored the same as or better than their male counterparts. The only trait in which women lagged men was envisioning—sensing opportunities and threats in the environment, setting strategic direction, and inspiring constituents. Although it may be a matter of perception, this lack stops women from getting to the top. Women who aspire to leadership will benefit greatly from developing envisioning skills.

THE PULL OF VISION ON TEAM PERFORMANCE

You hit an unexpected patch of black ice while driving down the highway and feel the car go into a skid. Adrenaline rushing, what do you do? The experts offer simple advice for that situation—*look* where you want the car to go. When you focus on the desired direction, your instincts take over and you'll do the right thing to guide the car through the skid.

Envisioning in business works much the same way. Focus on where you want to go. See it in your mind's eye, feel it in your body, hear the sounds associated with its fulfillment, smell and taste it. A clear vision of the future guides actions and decisions in a way that isn't possible when you are immersed in the distractions of present reality.

A sharply defined vision pulls you forward toward your objective, leading you through treacherous stretches. It guides you through inevitable breakdowns, resistance, and problems along the way, both external and internal. To strengthen the pull of the vision, find ways to inhabit your future dreams.

For example, if your personal moonshot is to climb the highest mountain in the world, go beyond visualizing the process of climbing and imagine the experience of standing at the top of Mount Everest. Imagine what you see, how you feel physically and emotionally, and who is present as you stand atop this peak. When you truly inhabit this future moment in your mind, the outcome becomes more real to you. Your neural circuits rehearse the situation, and it becomes part of your experience.

A similar thing happens when teams collaborate to create a shared vision of the future. As people imagine the future together, they discover clues to successful future teamwork. A strong vision pulls people toward a future in which they operate with greater effect.

66 Obstacles are those frightful things you see when you take your mind off your goals. 99

HENRY FORD

Travel to the Future

One way to get people on the same page for a future vision is to visualize, as a group, what happens when you complete the moonshot. Use the following exercise to close a planning session for your initiative.

Imagine that everyone on the team is together at the celebration after having successfully reached the goal. In this ideal future, acknowledge individuals on the team for their particular contributions to the team's success.

- Have everyone on the team take a moment to envision the after-party. Where is it held? What does the venue look like? What sounds can they hear? What can they smell? How do they feel having accomplished so much?

- Next, ask everyone to hear themselves being acknowledged for their contributions to this future.

- Ask everyone to write down what they imagined: "I was acknowledged for _____."

- Share these glimpses into the future with each other.

It illuminates how each member expects and intends to contribute.

Something interesting often happens during the exercise—the team itself is transformed, linked by a common vision. Individuals understand their roles in the shared future and how to work effectively as part of the team. They discover the broader possibilities that emerge through the pursuit of their moonshot. This exercise creates strong, motivated teams that work together well *as if they had already succeeded.*

Make It Visible

When possible, create a visible reminder of the vision to inspire yourself and others. The wooden Palm prototype made a personal vision tangible for the entire team. Find your own equivalent.

One team imagined its project making the cover of a major industry magazine. A designer in the group quickly mocked up that potential future magazine cover and posted it on the wall of the dedicated moon-shot conference room, reminding everyone of the vision they had shared together.

The aspirational magazine cover works only when people spend time inhabiting the future vision. The visual aid is a *reminder* of a potential outcome that a team shares, not a way to prod people into committing to something they haven't yet experienced.

RENEWING THE VISION

The pull of vision may be powerful, but it diminishes with time. Smart leaders refresh and sustain that vision, particularly when engaged on long-term initiatives.

In the world of business,
the status quo exerts a strong gravitation pull.

Kennedy's speech at Rice University, cited at the start this chapter, occurred more than a year after his initial Moonshot speech to Congress. He took frequent action to renew momentum and feed public enthusiasm for the long-term goal, often visiting the various facilities and teams who developed the Apollo 11 technologies.

Inspiring people is only the start. The chapters ahead discuss ways to structure the moonshot to maintain momentum and sustain support from the stakeholders. Remain alert to opportunities to feed the vision over time, and keep your eyes on the future possibilities even when present difficulties loom.

66 **People often say motivation doesn't last. Well, neither does bathing—that's why we recommend it daily.** 99

ZIG ZIGLAR

SUIT UP

Adopt the Leadership Stance

People look to their leaders to demonstrate strength, especially during times of trial and stress. Undertaking a moonshot will provide plenty of stress, so be ready to show up with strength and confidence.

Gene Kranz describes the powerful leadership style of Christopher Kraft, the flight director during the Mercury-Apollo missions and later director of Johnson Space Center:

> *During the mission, Kraft set the tone when we lost our composure. He knew that he could not show any uncertainty to his team. In the Mercury Control Center there was no room for displays of emotion . . . His message from the earliest Mercury days: "We were the visible point men for the program and we had to maintain a calm, professional, and confident image."*

Powerful leaders aren't only decisive in everyday interactions; they also remain calm and steadfast in times of stress. Strong leadership supports effective team operations under tight deadlines and when plans break down.

After the Apollo 1 accident in 1967, in which three astronauts died during a pre-launch test before the first manned launch, Webb took responsibility and addressed it publicly. He told the media, "We've always known that something like this was going to happen sooner or later. . . . Who would have thought that the first tragedy would be on the ground?"

Webb went to President Johnson and asked that NASA be allowed to handle the accident investigation, and to direct its recovery. He promised to be truthful in assessing blame and pledged to accept responsibility on behalf of himself and NASA management, as appropriate. As a result of Webb's handling of the investigation, both NASA's image and popular support were largely undamaged.

Sometimes situations demand a convincing performance, even when your confidence wanes. Adept leaders intentionally summon confidence, optimism, strength, and decisiveness so they can show up in a way that makes everyone more effective.

Learn to use body language, speech, and inner motivation to strengthen your confidence and composure.

THE STANCES OF POWER

Not feeling as confident as you might like? Change your body stance. How you stand or sit affects those around you. Surprisingly, it may also affect how you feel and behave.

People around you react to your physical presence on a subconscious level. And research has identifed "power stances" that both exude and promote power in social situations.

In a power stance, you take up *more* room than average, whether sitting or standing. Your arms are open, your chest and neck exposed. Picture Superman with his hands on his hips. In contrast, powerless poses minimize the space you occupy. Visualize someone slumping down in a chair, lowering the head, or crossing arms and legs tightly.

Your physical stance affects your inner landscape as well, changing the chemistry of your brain in subtle ways.

Research shows that certain hormone combinations contribute to leadership, for alpha animals in the wild and leaders in the boardroom alike. Individuals who occupy leadership roles tend to have higher testosterone levels relative to other people. Testosterone is associated with leadership and risk tolerance. They also exhibit lower levels of cortisol, the hormone associated with stress. The levels of these two key hormones fluctuate in response to external and internal stimuli.

In general, lowering cortisol while raising testosterone improves performance under stress. The good news is that you can do this without taking a single pill.

According to research conducted by Amy Cuddy, a social psychologist and professor at the Harvard Business School, adopting a power stance triggers hormonal shifts that characterize powerful leaders.

These power stances have the same effect in private, when you are alone in the office or sitting in the car. Use this fact your advantage before high-stakes, high-stress situations. According to Cuddy, when you spend as little as two minutes privately in a power stance, the resulting hormone adjustment improves your ability to handle stress and manage risks.

SPEAK WITH AUTHORITY

Pay close attention to your words when you speak to board members, executive teams, customer groups, and staff, both formally and informally.

Speak in a way that others hear leadership.

Start with the words themselves. Many people use filler words to buy time while they gather their thoughts. These verbal tics undermine authority. For example, the phrase "you know" impels the listener to provide support or affirmation, and thus saps the speaker's power.

People in power can afford to pause. They hold the floor with intention and are willing to take the time to gather their thoughts.

Some words and phrases diminish the certainty of statements, effectively draining power. For example:

- "I only want to . . ."

- "It's just that . . ."

- "I'd like to . . ."

- "I think . . ."

- "It seems like . . ."

- "In my opinion . . ."

Ironically, adding the word *very* for emphasis often weakens the overall meaning. Consider the following three statements:

- "I'm very happy." – The "very" sounds like you're insisting too much.

- "I'm happy." – Simpler is stronger in this case.

- "I'm thrilled." – Better yet, choose a stronger adjective.

How you speak is almost as important as what you say. Vocal inflection can undermine the message of the words.

English language speakers in particular should beware of the practice of ending sentences with an upward lilt, as if their sentences are questions. The only sure way to fix this pattern of *upspeak* is to notice it and intentionally practice speaking with a steady or descending inflection.

Like a dedicated actor, pay attention to how you deliver your lines.

WATCH THE GAP BETWEEN WHAT YOU SPEAK AND WHAT OTHERS HEAR

When you step into a new role, people may hear you differently than before.

Kate learned this the hard way in her first executive role. She was accustomed to participating in meetings in a collaborative and creative manner. When leading a team, she continued to offer suggestions and brainstorm ideas without fully realizing that, in her new role, those words carried special weight. She discovered that people spent time pursuing thoughts she had thrown in as creative suggestions; they interpreted her comments as requests or mandates.

When brainstorming, be clear that's what you're doing. Before you leave a brainstorming session, ask attendees what action items they will take away, in case a casual comment or suggestion of yours has indeed been interpreted as a request.

SPEAK LESS

As you choose your words carefully, you may find yourself speaking less. Remaining silent works well for many leaders; when they do speak, their words carry more weight.

Many powerful CEOs attend meetings in near silence, carefully watching and listening, occasionally asking questions for clarification, but otherwise remaining silent.

When you choose not to speak you truly listen.

Silence allows you to hear and observe others around you, inevitably leading to better insight and leadership.

Powerful silence may be particularly important for women in leadership positions. According to research by Victoria Brescoll, a psychology professor at Yale University, women in high positions who talk more than others around them are perceived as *less* competent than their male peers.

All leaders benefit when they prune unnecessary words from their speech, get to the point, and listen carefully.

CONFIDENCE

When pursuing moonshots, leaders face daunting challenges and trying circumstances. When your confidence wanes, find strength from within.

According to Daniel Pink's book *To Sell Is Human*, interrogative self-talk is remarkably effective at enhancing performance in difficult situations. Begin an inner Q&A session. Ask yourself questions about *why* you will do well, and then answer them.

The internal dialog before a presentation to the board might sound like this:

- "Can I convince the board they need to invest?"

- "Yes, I've practiced my pitch and I understand their concerns. I know how to address their objections, and can get them excited about the outcome. I've prepared well. In the past I've rushed right into the data, but this time I will lead with a story and take a deep breath before I begin."

As you work through the situation, recall past experiences in which you have had success, and draw strength from them.

POWER WITHOUT THE PREP

Being prepared boosts confidence, but preparation can quickly tip into unhealthy perfectionism. Over-preparation is a crutch that actually can hold you back from recognizing and accepting opportunities. If nothing else, over-preparation may contribute to fatigue and burnout, and those who rely too heavily on preparation may lack agility when the situation requires them to think on their feet. Consider it as an expression of obsessive discipline that can morph into a self-imposed boundary.

If over-preparation is your path to confidence, find opportunities to exercise a *lack* of preparedness. That's right—prepare to be unprepared. Depend instead on your creativity. Improvise.

Be open with others around you: "I have not prepared for this meeting—how would you like me to contribute?"

Many powerful leaders use this technique to great effect.

You owe it to those who work for you to show up with confidence and composure as a leader. Their needs trump your personal comfort. As Webb and Kraft demonstrated in the Apollo 11 mission, being an effective and confident leader is the ultimate goal.

SECURE AN EXPLICIT COMMITMENT

Mission Approved

To get off the ground, a moonshot requires approval and resources. In 1961, President Kennedy asked Congress for between $7 billion and $9 billion over the following five years. Adjusted for inflation, that's between $55 billion and $72 billion in 2015 dollars. Those first allocations were the tip of the financial iceberg. According to NASA, the Apollo program spent more than $21 billion—the equivalent of $150 billion today—through the first lunar landing in 1969. That number does *not* include the Gemini and Mercury missions (which preceded Apollo), both instrumental in the long-term project.

The president needed Congress to approve budgets to get the mission started. As the program continued, the Apollo 11 team would need to win the support of different administrations time and again to secure a commitment of resources.

The first phase of a moonshot is getting an explicit commitment. A well-crafted pitch can help get the job done quickly.

SEIZING THE CRITICAL MOMENTS

In 2003, mobile phone adoption was on the brink of explosive growth, and online sales would account for a major part of the sales in years to come. In that pivotal year, AT&T Wireless seized market leadership by creating a groundbreaking online shopping site for users of its phones. Customers loved the novel shopping experience, and the company dominated online cell phone sales for years to come.

Moves like this look brilliant in hindsight. At the outset, however, the people involved often struggle to convince others to invest in a bold vision. In this story, the new head of the Mobile Consumer business unit's vision and pitch were instrumental to the company's ongoing success.

A client we'll call Joe was hired specifically to head the company's online sales of mobile phones. At the time, the company led the market in retail store cell phone sales but lagged the competition in the online channel.

Within days of joining the company, Joe realized the magnitude of the problem. The business wasn't close to achieving parity with its competitors' online sales channels, much less surpassing them.

To stake out a marketing-leading position, Joe knew the company had to far exceed what its competitors were doing. He completely reimagined the experience of shopping for a phone online. But this approach would require the company to reengineer its infrastructure and redesign business processes. The project would require an investment of $30 million in the first year, and more than $100 million over three years. This was *four times* the budget allocated for the online sales channel.

Joe needed a fast commitment. Without the funding, he could not fulfill his mandate. In hindsight, we know that the timing was critical for the company as well. With quick action, it could establish a strong presence while the market was still emerging.

Joe's urgency paid off, and the envisioned shopping experience became reality.

In the rest of this chapter, we'll explore what led to Joe's success: create urgency, share a compelling vision, and deliver a hole-in-one pitch.

CREATE URGENCY

Having identified a moonshot and communicated the vision, your task is to get buy-in for your idea quickly, so you can maintain urgency and excitement.

Important initiatives that lack urgency end up
on the back burner.

Because they swim against the stream of business as usual, moonshots fight the drag of doubt and delay. Fear and uncertainty often doom bold projects to lower-level committees for evaluation until the excitement wanes. And indifference is not the caliber of rocket fuel needed to launch an idea into the stratosphere—and beyond.

To secure resources or approval for a moonshot, work quickly to get people on board before inertia sets in. Getting approval from key stakeholders isn't a matter of how carefully you prepare your slides or how well you speak. On the flip side, having a good idea is essential, but not enough to get buy-in.

Success depends on creating a sense of urgency in the people you pitch. It's the *hole-in-one pitch* formula that often results in quick approvals.

A HOLE-IN-ONE PITCH

When you guide others to feel the pull of the vision, you increase the chances of gaining a commitment in a single meeting: a "hole in one."

A hole-in-one pitch follows a specific pattern. Start by getting agreement on the current situation. Next, focus on the outcome and the *experience* of the desired outcome. Having explored the desired experience, describe your proposed solution, handle any objections, and then ask for a commitment.

The seemingly quick success requires groundwork and preparation.

We will refer to the people you meet with as the *audience*, since this technique works equally well with individuals or groups—such as boards. Listen carefully to your audience and integrate their perspectives as you progress through the phases of the pitch.

When getting approval from a group, you may cycle through this process several times with individual pre-meetings in advance of the main event. For example, to gain approval from the board of directors, meet individually with a few of the directors to secure their advice and agreement ahead of time. Refine your pitch using their input. In this way you enlist them as your allies because they're invested in your success, and see their success tied to yours. By the time you get to the board meeting, you'll have the necessary support and will be prepared to secure an immediate commitment.

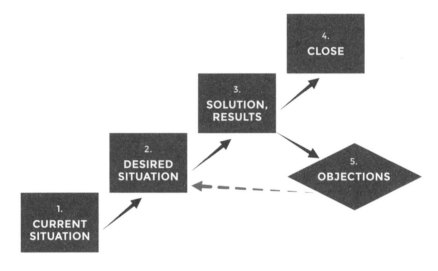

LINING UP FOR A HOLE-IN-ONE MEETING

Here's how to move from proposal to commitment in a single meeting. For informal pre-meetings, make the following process a discussion, not a presentation.

- **THE CURRENT SITUATION:** What are the current pains and unmet needs? Present facts, not opinions.

- **OUTCOME AND DESIRED EXPERIENCE:** What does the business look like in the future when the problem is solved? What is now possible that was not possible before? Paint a compelling picture of future possibilities.

- **SOLUTION AND RESULTS:** How do you propose to go from the current situation to the desired experience? Describe the plan and activities to achieve the desired outcome and results.

- **THE CLOSE:** When the audience is sold on the outcome, ask for a verbal commitment for the next step. Be specific.

- **OBJECTIONS (IF ANY):** Acknowledge objections. Reframe them as challenges that are worth overcoming in order to achieve the desired experience and future outcomes.

Where possible, *show rather than tell*. Invite the audience to experience the current situation or future outcome with you.

1. The Current Situation

The first step is exploring the current situation. Discuss current problems and unmet needs while remaining grounded in hard facts.

Don't assume that you understand the audience's priorities and needs. Ask open-ended questions to reveal specifics about the current situation as it relates to your proposal. Craft questions using the following as guides:

- What are your top priorities for [your topic here]? What is the reality today?

- What is working well in this area today? What's not working well?

- If you keep going with what you're doing today, will you be able to reach your objectives?

To stay grounded in facts, don't say, for example, that your current product interface is terrible: that is your *opinion*. Instead say, "Our most important customers give us a low score on the product interface. Their specific words were . . ." Those are facts, not your opinions.

> **THE CURRENT SITUATION:** At the telecom company board meeting, Joe demonstrated the process of purchasing a cell phone on the company's own site and its competitors' sites. The board members experienced the reality of the company's poor online experience directly. Joe illustrated the pain from the customer's perspective, without stating his opinion.

2. The Outcome and Desired Experience

Having determined and demonstrated the problem, the next step is to paint the picture of a different future. Focus on the *outcome* of the proposal, not details.

Guide the conversation so that listeners themselves suggest the potential benefits of solving the problem. Depending on your audience, use questions such as the following:

- What will it mean to the business as a whole when we solve this problem?

- What will it mean to customers? Shareholders?

- In a future with this problem addressed, what is now possible in our business? Does this change present new business opportunities?

- What will be possible for you personally and your team?

- How will the board of directors and the investors feel about this outcome?

- How does this outcome compare with the path we are on today?

Pay close attention to the specific words people choose to answer these questions. Words offer insight into what people value. Encourage them to imagine—experience via visualization—what the situation would be like when the problem is solved.

> **THE DESIRED SITUATION:** Joe predicted that if mobile phones followed the pattern of other products, 30 percent of all phones would be sold on the Internet within three years. Without a viable online store, the company could lose 10 percent or more of its market share, representing $300 million in sales. On the other hand, if the company created this breakthrough web experience, it could become the leader in online sales within a year–a market share increase of 5 to 10 percent in the first year. Board members could rally around that future outcome.

3. The Solution and Result

Finally, it's time to talk about your proposal.

Wait—don't launch into a pre-packaged pitch. Having listened carefully in the previous two steps, you now understand how the audience perceives the problem and how they might experience a better future. Your task is to build the bridge between their perception of the current situation and that desired future. Echo the key words and phrases people used as a way of demonstrating that you have heard their concerns. This can also enhance a sense of connection by implying that you value what they value.

> **THE SOLUTION AND RESULTS:** In the board meeting, Joe demonstrated a mock-up of the radically reinvented online buying experience. When he clicked on the phone, the image rotated 360 degrees to deliver a full view of the device. In 2003, most e-tail sites were basically online brochures, cluttered with static, two-dimensional pictures and loads of text. But Joe was showing something entirely different, something that went beyond what the board could imagine. The purchase experience surpassed that of the competition, offering capabilities the executive team didn't even know were possible. Joe then presented the budget and resource requirements, and a timeline to launch the new site before the holiday buying season—creating urgency.

4. Time the Close

Having laid the groundwork as described above, the close is usually a foregone conclusion. Summarize how your proposal addresses the problems of the current situation and leads to the desired experience. Describe the cost and implementation timing, then make a specific request for commitment and outline the next steps. For example:

- Will you call Sue to let her know that we've discussed this, and you support my plan?

- When the executive committee meets, will you vote to approve a $30 million budget for phase one?

- Will you approve my request for two additional staff to support this project next quarter?

- Will you set up a meeting with John to discuss this project and gain his commitment to assign two of his team members, Susan and Frank, to the project for 90 days?

- Will you approve the budget to hire the web design firm to refresh and relaunch our web presence?

> **THE CLOSE:** Once the board was excited about the reinvented online shopping experience, Joe closed by summarizing the potential market share gain and return on investment. He reminded them how increasing market share and delivering a breakthrough web experience could affect analyst ratings and the company's stock price. Joe then made a clear request, asking the board to approve $30 million immediately and $100 million over three years.

5. Handle Objections

Address any objections by returning to the anticipated results and desired experience. If you listen carefully, you may discover objections that you will encounter later.

Objections often fall into two categories: budget and process.

"We don't have the budget for this." Budget objections result from a mismatch between the perceived value and the investment. If a proposal is compelling, people will shift budget from other areas. While it may be tempting to pull out a Return on Investment (ROI) analysis when you hear cost concerns, revisit the potential outcomes and the benefits to the business. Focus on selling the desired experience and the value that the solution will provide. Return to big-picture questions like:

- What will be possible in the business if we take this course?

- What happens if we don't act on this now and let the opportunity pass? Can we reach our goals with business as usual?

- What if our competitors act and we don't? What will happen to our business?

- Where can we find budget allocation that is less critical to the business, where we might be able to defer spending? How else can we free up budget to fund this initiative?

When facing pushback about the millions needed for the lunar mission, President Lyndon B. Johnson, Kennedy's successor, apparently asked legislators: "Would you rather have us be a second-rate nation, or should we spend a little money?"

Process-based objections occur when the listener mentally starts down the path to the future and encounters a problem or roadblock. Try to have people imagine a future in which they have solved this objection, and listen for other potential objections you may hear. Respond with a positive tone that indicates you have heard their concerns but still want to press ahead toward the new, better future that will result from your project.

"We don't know how we'll do it yet, but let's assume that we can solve that problem. Can we move forward? What else will we need to address along the way?"

In Joe's situation, the board immediately approved the $30 million budget request in a single meeting—an unprecedented action. The rest is telecommunications history.

MAINTAIN THE SUPPLY LINES

The Art of Managing Up

The years between 1961 and 1969, between the declaration of the Moonshot and the actual lunar landing, spanned three presidential administrations. Each administration recommitted to the effort.

Those years were filled with social unrest in the United States. The manned moon mission faced plenty of opposition and competing funding priorities. Many scientists considered the deadline rushed and unrealistic. Others in Congress and beyond wanted to invest the money domestically, rather than in space.

The success of the original Moonshot was due, in part, to the ongoing efforts of James Webb, the head of NASA from 1961 to 1968. He worked closely with three presidents and reported directly to congressional committees. As previously mentioned, after the launchpad fire that claimed the lives of three crew members, he personally updated the congressional committee about the ongoing investigation into the tragedy. NASA's biography of Webb describes the man and his accomplishments in the following brief bio:

> *For seven years after President Kennedy's May 25, 1961, lunar landing announcement, through October 1968, James Webb politicked, coaxed, cajoled, and maneuvered for NASA in Washington. As a longtime Washington insider he was a master at bureaucratic politics.*

James Webb was a visionary leader who regularly practiced communicating up.

COMMUNICATING UP

Long-term support for a moonshot requires consistent, effective communication with stakeholders.

By signing off on a moonshot, a leadership team accepts a significant risk. You owe it to board members, investors, and other advocates to update them with the information they need to sustain their support.

> *The most effective leaders are adept at the art of managing up.*

Too often, upward communications slide down the list of priorities. In the rush of working on a moonshot, execution demands your attention. You're busy, and you're on a roll.

By communicating regularly and effectively with supporters and stakeholders, you improve the odds of long-term success.

Here are four reasons to invest time and energy in upward communications:

- **ENSURE THAT CONTRIBUTIONS ARE RECOGNIZED.** Give your team's accomplishments and your team leaders the visibility they deserve.

- **KEEP THE MOONSHOT ON THE RADAR.** Regular updates maintain the focus on the moonshot and its potential outcome and benefits.

- **TURN SUPPORTERS INTO ADVOCATES.** Others have gone out on a limb to support the objective. Give them information to champion successes, answer questions, and defend their positions. Any successes reflect positively on your supporters; provide information they can easily share.

- **AVOID SURPRISES.** If there's a potential problem, point it out and tell people what you're doing about it. Executives and boards of directors hate surprises. It's better to address potential problems and their solutions head-on than to lose trust when problems arise.

Cultivating the art of managing up brings personal benefits as well. Effective communication elevates your stature within an organization. The ability to distill and summarize important details and maintain a future focus separates a leader from a manager. To elevate your leadership, deliver concise, high-level communication framed in the context of future success and possibility.

In September of 2014, the CEO of a large consumer products company was notified that surplus monies would be made available for an innovative project, and all of the parent company's business entities were invited to submit proposals. Amy, the senior vice-president of sales, decided to propose an idea for an innovative marketing campaign. She knew that if she prepared a proposal that her CEO would not need to rework prior to submission, it would be submitted quickly, and that would improve chances of winning the funds. Rather than laboring over an extensive proposal, Amy prepared an executive summary–style presentation. It was results-oriented rather than process-oriented, and included estimates of the impact of the campaign and the return on investment. The presentation was just five pages, and Amy turned it around in less than an hour and sent it to her CEO, who submitted it immediately. By 5 p.m. that same day, Amy's CEO informed her that they had been awarded the funds.

The next day Amy discovered that nobody else had even submitted a competing proposal—several leaders in other subsidiaries were busy working on big, complicated presentations and completely missed the opportunity. The proposal review team was so impressed by her responsiveness and the quality of what had been submitted that they granted the funds immediately, seeing no need to wait on other ideas. The instinct to create a concise and compelling proposal and to be highly responsive proved to be the winning strategy. When the decision was announced, the other teams requested that Amy send them her proposal for insight into how to create a compelling, board-worthy business case.

HOW COMMUNICATING UP IS DIFFERENT

When framing communications for high-level executives, consider how you can be effective given the unique constraints and realities of their roles.

TIME CONSTRAINTS: Top-level executives and directors juggle unrelenting demands. Securing a large chunk of time with a C-level executive or board of directors is nearly impossible. Be concise and plan for interruptions.

LINEAR VS. NON-LINEAR THINKING: Many people in leadership positions are *non-linear thinkers*. They start with the big picture, then fill in the details, rather than progressing through points in a linear fashion to reach a conclusion. Match your communication to this thinking style.

PRIORITIES AND CONTEXT: CEOs, boards, and investors operate within a broad business context. When speaking with the board or investors, understand their priorities and objectives. What looks huge to you may seem trivial to them.

Filter what you report to include only the most crucial information. The higher people are in an organization, the less they want to deal with details. Do not simply forward e-mails and imagine that you've communicated effectively. Flooding your superiors with information generally proves ineffective and may be annoying. Unless there's a problem that requires their attention, assume that they trust you to manage the details.

SUMMARY FIRST, DETAILS UPON REQUEST

When updating people in high-level positions, communicate in a way that respects their perspectives and the demands on their time.

Start by summarizing what the executive needs to know at that moment. Identify the essential takeaways, which may include potential problems or specific requests. Keep the details on standby and lead with the most important points.

This format applies to both written and spoken communications.

For in-person meetings, spend time in advance identifying the important things you want to communicate. Ideally, keep the list to no more than three points.

For example, a moonshot status update for a CEO might sound like this:

- We're on target for meeting the July launch date. (She can relay this important status information to others.)

- We're having a problem getting partner A to agree to our dates, but I will have it resolved in a week. If not, I'll let you know. (This heads-up about a potential issue prevents surprises down the road.)

- Russ in finance is worried about the expense impact of this initiative. Here are three things I ask that you communicate to him to show your support and address his concerns. (If you have a specific request, make it clearly.)

Then let the CEO ask for more details on any issue.

Written communications follow the same format. If necessary, spend the time to draft a communication for this purpose, and have a colleague review it. It's a worthwhile investment.

Summarize so that others focus on wins, specific requests, or proposed solutions to problems.

If you think of the communication as a story, start with the ending and use it to build curiosity about the path that got you there. If you have piqued the person's interest, you may be asked about how you reached that point:

- "We found a way to double our new enrollments with a $10,000 investment."

- "The team has solved the customer issue and we're ready to meet the next milestone."

PUTTING IT ALL TOGETHER: SEVEN STEPS TO COMMUNICATING UP

1. Be Concise and Lead with the Summary

Lead with a few key pieces of information the reader or listener needs to know. Drop into detail only when asked to do so. Whether you're talking to a CEO or a board, interruptions are common. Always start with three key points in case that's all you have time to cover.

2. Speak Clearly and Plainly

Using industry jargon or vague terms distracts your listeners from the essential message because they'll waste brain cycles trying to decipher what you're saying. Translate arcane terms and details into relevant information.

3. Be Relevant

What are the top concerns of your audience, whether it's the board, investors, CEOs, or other key influencers? Your CEO may have three to five top-level outcomes for the business (growth, profitability, customer satisfaction, entering new markets, etc.). If possible, reinforce how your moonshot contributes to important priorities.

4. Be Bold

Take a stand and make recommendations. If you see a potential problem, don't simply present the problem. Describe the steps you're taking to resolve it, or recommend a course of action.

5. Be Specific in Requests

Decide in advance what you want as a result of the meeting and ask for it specifically.

6. Reframe Results as Possibilities

Remind listeners about potential outcomes and possibilities of success. Keep renewing the inspiration that garnered support in the first place.

7. Be Consistent

Make it clear that this is an ongoing communication. Let them know when they can expect to hear from you again. Find out how often they want to hear updates. For example:

- I'll send another update in two weeks.

- Once we hear from the partner next month, I'll let you know if we're still on schedule.

Put the follow-up on your calendar. Earn ongoing trust by making commitments and sticking to them consistently.

Here is an example of an effective communication string from a startup CEO to a member of his board of directors.

SUBJECT:
STATUS OF OUR BETA PRODUCT RELEASE

We missed our July 1 deadline. We've identified that our planning process was broken and have taken steps to correct it and to get our development process back on track.

- **PROBLEM:** Our plans did not contain sufficient detail or intermediate deadlines. Because of this we didn't realize we were behind until our deadline was upon us, and missed opportunities to make early course corrections.

- **SOLUTION:** We've added the identification of key assumptions and checkpoints that can be tracked objectively to our planning process. We now validate our assumptions as early as possible and monitor progress on a daily basis.

- **RESULT:** While reworking the software this past month, we identified key speed and quantity assumptions, validated them, and were successful in planning for and hitting a target completion date two weeks out. We are using the same approach for planning our next product release.

SCHEDULED REFLECTION

The busier we are, the less we tend to stop and think. Setting aside regular periods to craft upward communications is one way to build time for reflection into your schedule.

Research shows that taking time for reflection improves both productivity and learning. In a study of tech support call center trainees, people who spent 15 minutes each day reflecting on their training significantly outperformed those who spent the additional 15 minutes working on the training.

As you schedule time to craft communications for managing up, you benefit from the time spent in reflection.

INTENTIONAL AND REGULAR COMMUNICATIONS

Establish a process to maintain consistent upward communications.

- Who will receive updates? You might have multiple stakeholders.

- How often do they want updates?

- What's their preferred format? Do they need any special formats or types of data?

- What's the nature of their support (status, guidance, etc.)?

Use this information to create a plan for regular communications, as if creating an editorial calendar.

Include these updates in your project calendar. Dedicate time and identify resources if you want assistance preparing data or graphics. Scheduling updates prevents emergencies later on.

USE "SO THAT" TO ELEVATE YOUR IMPACT

Frame activities and contributions in the broader context of possibilities using the "so that" technique. Before you next communicate up, go through the following exercise:

- Make a list of results you have produced in the last month.

- Turn the results into broader accomplishments by adding "so that" or "which makes it possible to" at the end of each.

- For example:

  » "After a lengthy negotiation, we signed the partnership agreement with Acme, which makes it possible for us to enter two new markets."

» "We solved the technical problem that delayed the beta, so that we can now ship. In doing so, we created quality assurance and troubleshooting techniques so that in the future we can spot problems much earlier in the development cycle."

Whether you're reporting status, problems, or breakthroughs, future context gives advocates and others reasons to support your moonshot.

THE POWER OF ACKNOWLEDGMENT

Cultivate Leadership by Giving Credit

The celebrated architect Frank Lloyd Wright left an imprint on American architecture. His legacy, however, did not extend to those who worked closely with him. The notoriously difficult architect insisted that his own name appear atop their work, refusing to acknowledge their contributions. Few of his apprentices constructed successful architectural careers of their own. He built buildings, not careers.

Some leaders elevate the performance of those around them. One way to achieve this is through consistent and thoughtful acknowledgment of the efforts of others.

Meaningful acknowledgment is the fuel that drives individual and team performance. When people trust that their contributions are seen and valued, they are motivated to make an extra effort.

Neil Armstrong was the public hero behind the Apollo 11 mission. Yet he was always modest and quick to acknowledge the efforts of the vast team behind the scenes that made the moon landing possible.

"When you have hundreds of thousands of people all doing their job a little better than they have to, you get an improvement in performance," Armstrong said in a NASA oral history interview in 2001. "And that's the only reason we could have pulled this whole thing off."

Like many of the practices described in this book, acknowledgment is something that we *think* we do. Yet it is often lost in the everyday demands of business as usual. We assume that others *know* we appreciate their efforts, even when we don't specifically acknowledge them.

Consistently acknowledging the efforts of those around you creates a culture in which people's contributions are both noted and appreciated. When undertaking a moonshot, acknowledgment serves as essential fuel.

Leaders who consistently acknowledge others are the ones who people follow across teams and organizations.

During his 10-year career as the CEO of Campbell's Soup, Douglas Conant wrote many thousands of thank-you notes to employees, actively acknowledging their successes and contributions. Obviously, he had a host of other pressing things to do. But he understood the power of acknowledgment to the success of the company.

Leaders who fail to acknowledge employee contributions endanger their own effectiveness. According to a 2015 Harris/Interact poll of 1,000 workers, people considered "not recognizing employee achievements" as a barrier to effective leadership.

THE FOUR LEVELS OF ACKNOWLEDGMENT

Handing out praise is the simplest but least powerful form of acknowledgment. Praise can be insincere. By *acknowledgment,* we mean both observation and gratitude.

In the business context, you can recognize an individual's contribution at one of four levels.

- **LEVEL ONE:** About the thing

- **LEVEL TWO:** About the person who did the thing

- **LEVEL THREE:** About the personal impact of the person/thing

- **LEVEL FOUR:** About the broader impact of the person's contribution

The impact of acknowledgment increases dramatically with each level. The deeper the level, the more it cements team loyalty.

Acknowledgment fuels passion and involvement.

Level One: About the Thing

The simplest and most common type of acknowledgment is to call out someone's action or contribution, publicly and positively. Healthy work environments are filled with this kind of acknowledgment.

- "That was a terrific presentation."

- "Good work shipping the beta on time."

- "Thank you for the thorough analysis."

In informal terms, a level-one acknowledgment is rather like telling someone "nice tie!" It costs the giver little in terms of thought or effort. Although people are gratified to hear the praise, its effect dissipates quickly.

Even this simple type of recognition is conspicuously absent in many business environments.

Level Two: About the Person

To magnify the impact of an acknowledgment, make it about the *person* you're recognizing rather than, or in addition to, the result.

Using the "nice tie" analogy, a level-two acknowledgment calls out both the tie and the wearer's impeccable taste and care in selecting neckwear. This type of comment is like holding up a mirror so recipients can see themselves from others' perspectives.

Here are a few examples, building on the easy, level-one acknowledgments above:

- "I loved your presentation. You were clearly prepared, and your personal stories were memorable and gave your presentation more impact."

- "Congratulations for shipping the beta on time. You showed tremendous resourcefulness and determination when you worked through those show-stopping problems and found solutions quickly enough to get the product out on schedule."

- "Thank you for the thorough analysis. You have really helped us to better understand our customers."

Delivering this kind of personal comment requires thought and attention. It demonstrates that the recipient's efforts are both noticed and appreciated. These interactions build the foundation for good working relationships.

Level Three: About the Personal Impact

The third type of acknowledgment goes deeper by acknowledging not only the action and the person, but also the person's impact on you.

- "I loved your presentation. You were clearly prepared, and your personal stories were memorable and gave your presentation more impact. You have inspired me to change the way I do presentations to include personal stories."

- "Congratulations for shipping the beta on time. You showed tremendous resourcefulness and determination when you worked through those show-stopping problems and found solutions quickly enough to get the product out on schedule. You've convinced me that we need to streamline the release processes. I'd love your input on how to do that for future releases."

- "Thank you for the thorough analysis. You have really helped us to better understand our customers. I am creating a new product concept and now see how important it is to include in-depth customer research; do you want to be part of it?"

If you have ever received an acknowledgment at this level, you remember it. It has a deep, personal impact.

These comments build loyalty and sustain relationships. Teams that interact with each other in this way work together better and find work more rewarding. This kind of acknowledgment is like rocket fuel for motivation.

Delivering an authentic level-three acknowledgment requires work and reflection. That preparation contributes to the value of the practice. When you think deeply about others' contributions and their impact, you'll engage with them differently. You'll discover what works well in teams and relationships, and that perspective changes the climate around you in a positive way.

A WORD OF CAUTION: You cannot fake it when giving these acknowledgments. If you don't genuinely mean what you say, your voice or body language will betray that fact. You will then lose credibility and damage trust, rather than build loyalty.

If you cannot come up with an authentic comment for an individual, think more deeply about that person's efforts and perspective. The practice of acknowledgment develops empathy, which is key to effective leadership and team communications.

Level Four: About the Broader Impact

There's a fourth level of acknowledgment—recognizing the contribution of the individual to the team, the business, or the world at large. A level-four acknowledgment turns the individual into a hero for a larger group.

This type of recognition is fairly rare. Only leaders confident in their own roles do the work to give glory to others.

Letting people know that they have changed the world, even in some small way, is a precious gift. Teams that celebrate heroes are strengthened by shared values and vision.

THE HERO OF THE RED CHAIR
What can an executive assistant teach executives?
Plenty, if you're paying attention.

Neil Vogel, CEO of New York-based About.com, took his executive team to an off-site retreat at a remote location: an isolated hotel in the Hamptons, a three-hour drive from New York City. The day before the retreat, the executive assistant, Tatum, arrived to check the meeting room. And she found a major problem.

Instead of the comfortable executive chairs pictured on the hotel's website, the conference room was filled with folding chairs. Uncomfortable chairs would not work for an all-day meeting. Thus began the journey to solving the problem, and the contest between Tatum's determination and the business-as-usual attitude of the venue's meeting representative.

The hotel could not satisfy Tatum's requirements. It didn't have better chairs; no one nearby had better chairs to rent or borrow. It was late in the day, and the meeting started the next morning. After hearing all the reasons why the hotel could not solve the chair problem, Tatum took charge. She ordered chairs from an office supply store in Manhattan. She contracted with a transportation company to pick up the chairs from the store, packaged in flat boxes, and deliver them to the hotel's location by 8:30 that night. She spoke directly with the hotel's maintenance manager, who scheduled an off-duty engineer to assemble the chairs overnight. At 9:30 that evening, Tatum checked on the first assembled chair, and she was there early the next morning to verify that the chairs were ready for the meeting.

The team arrived to find the conference room set up with a pristine white conference table, surrounded by fire-engine red leather chairs. The chairs were the visual highlight of the room, and comfortable as well. The attendees loved them.

The chairs would have disappeared into history (and company storage) except that Tatum was invited into the meeting to share the story of how the chairs got there. The team learned of her repeated efforts to bypass resistance, her attention to detail, and her creativity in solving the problem.

When the team was asked to acknowledge the person who had made the greatest contribution to the business during the off-site, the VP of Sales chose Tatum. In her, he saw the drive and commitment that he wanted his own sales team to have, and vowed to share her story with his team back at the office. Two days later, the CEO called an all-hands meeting to share the vision and strategies resulting from the off-site meeting. He led with the "Red Chair" story. The red chairs have since become a symbol for the team of inventive solutions that are not deterred by the drag of the everyday.

By paying attention, you can find heroic action in unexpected places and turn extraordinary effort into inspiration.

LEADING DIFFICULT CONVERSATIONS WITH ACKNOWLEDGMENT

Starting a difficult conversation with a genuine acknowledgment defuses defensiveness so that the recipient can absorb your message and a real conversation can emerge. This practice can be vitally important in difficult, emotionally loaded situations, reestablishing the trust you have built in the relationship to this point.

For example, if someone on your team objects to spending money hiring outside resources to make a milestone deadline for the moonshot, take the time to understand and recognize the strength and value of the person's perspective.

"Your financial analysis of the situation is quite thorough, and I respect your commitment to using our resources carefully. And while I agree this proposal will increase cost, the investment is essential to reducing risk in the project, and I know it will pay off by preventing cost overruns due to project delays. For this reason I ask that you reconsider your position . . . "

We are not advocating sugarcoating problems in a conversation. But starting the discussion with a genuine acknowledgment begins the conversation on a constructive note rather than a confrontational one. Often this opens the door to a faster resolution.

THE ACKNOWLEDGMENT QUOTA

Give yourself a quota for acknowledgments each week—and act on it. Once you start looking for reasons to recognize your team and peers, it becomes a habit. You will improve your ability to see team member contributions, increasing the quality of your interactions with others.

- **WEEK 1:** Deliver at least one acknowledgment in every meeting you attend. If you're stumped about what to say, listen carefully during the meeting to find something worth noting. "George just had a terrific insight. I'd never thought of the issue that way. Thanks, George."

- **WEEK 2:** Set a quota of three acknowledgments a day, and one level-three acknowledgment per week.

Track the acknowledgments you give and pay attention to what happens. Does the mood in the room change? Do people interact with you differently? Did it lead to unexpected or unusual conversations?

When you give a level-two or level-three acknowledgment, note the person's reaction. In most cases, you'll know immediately if the comment has landed and had a positive impact. Generous and sincere gratitude brings benefits to both the giver and the receiver.

ELEVATE YOUR PEOPLE SKILLS

Actions that Build and Maintain Rapport

Logs of the frequent communications between the Command Center in Houston and the Apollo 11 crew in space reveal friendly banter alongside the critical instructions and updates. Flight controllers would read news and sports reports to the men in space. Astronauts would welcome the next group of specialists as they began their shifts at Mission Control in Houston, crack jokes, and talk about the food.

> **APOLLO 11:** Down in the control center you might want to join us in wishing Dr. George Mueller a happy birthday.
>
> **CC:** Roger. We are standing by for your birthday greetings.
>
> **APOLLO 11:** I think today is also the birthday of California, and I believe they are 200 years old, and we send them a happy birthday. And I think it's Dr. Mueller's birthday, also, and don't think he is that old.

The space crew would share their wildly different perspectives of the weather, with the astronauts reporting on weather systems they could see approaching Houston.

It is essential that people living in tight quarters get along with each other. The astronauts and flight controllers alike understood that the mission depended on their ability to work together and build trust. They continuously invested in developing rapport, even under extreme conditions.

When leading others on a moonshot, building and maintaining rapport pays solid dividends. The leaders we work with intentionally create tight working conditions to strengthen the ties between members of their teams. They often sequester the core team, moving them into a new office in which they design their new work environment. For people to abandon the safety of business as usual, they must get to know, like, and trust each other.

DEVELOP PEOPLE SKILLS

Some people put others at ease immediately and are adept at initiating conversations. They make others feel seen and remembered.

Are these individuals blessed with innate people skills that build rapport and cultivate loyalty from those around them? Is the gift of being instantly likeable something you're born with?

Yes and no.

Early in our lives, we develop systems for connecting with each other, deciding whether to trust someone, and liking others. Some people are naturally skilled at tapping into those mental and social systems. But the methods of building rapport can be cultivated at any age.

The ability to connect with people quickly is important to every leader. You don't get much done in business without other people. Because pursuing a moonshot asks those around you to follow you and take risks, earning trust is critical.

Think you're too busy to worry about the "soft skills" of getting people to like you? Wrong. Leaders who know how to create and maintain rapport *save* time, because teams act with greater confidence and operate more effectively in an environment based on trust.

HOW ARE WE ALIKE? THE SEARCH FOR AFFINITY

Cognitive science suggests that our minds are complex places, often operating outside of the realm of rationality. Behavioral economist and Nobel Prize winner Daniel Kahneman describes our minds as using two systems when making decisions.

- **SYSTEM 1** is our intuition or automatic mental system, which relies on shortcuts and heuristics to make decisions quickly. System 1 is also responsible for reading social situations and forming impressions.

- **SYSTEM 2** is the reasoning and rational mind—the one that thinks through problems using reason, and deploys focused attention.

Driving to work every day becomes a System 1 activity for many people, who listen to the radio or an audiobook while behind the wheel. If someone asks you for detailed directions to your workplace, you call on the focus and effort of System 2 to provide clear directions.

We depend on System 1 for survival. We don't have enough mental energy to apply rational decisions to everything in our lives. System 1 generates our *first impressions*, which shape our decisions and behavior in ways that are generally appropriate. We also use System 1 to quickly assess whether a situation presents a threat. This skill was vital for our ancestors living in the wild, but it creates problems in today's business environment.

Have you ever tried to start a discussion or difficult conversation with reason and rationality, only to have it fall flat? You were appealing to the other person's System 2 mind. If you want people to invest the mental effort to think through your arguments, you must get past the intuitive gatekeeper, which is programmed to avoid threats from the outside.

Moonshots disrupt the status quo and may be perceived as threats. That's why it's essential to build rapport.

To build a productive working relationship, learn how to set people's emotional, intuitive minds at ease. The fastest way to do this is to find and reinforce points of similarity at three different levels:

1. Mirror body language

2. Echo key words to create resonance

3. Create narrative connections with "small talk"

Use these strategies to convert a skeptical or neutral colleague into an ally and maintain smooth working relationships with team members.

MIRROR BODY LANGUAGE FOR ALIGNMENT

The first technique, strategic mirroring, works with the so-called reptilian brain, which constantly scans for threats. This part of your brain perceives someone who is different from you as a potential threat. By mirroring an individual's body language, you subconsciously signal that you share the same outlook as the person you are speaking with, and participate in the same tribe.

For many of us, mirroring is so intuitive that it happens without us realizing we're doing it. If you're in an intense conversation with someone and she leans toward you, you often lean in yourself, almost instinctively.

However, body language mirroring may shut down in business situations, particularly when we're distracted with other concerns or not truly present in the conversation. Even if you think you're texting discreetly during a meeting, your body language betrays the fact that you're not present.

When a conversation is not going as you'd like, you can realign how you sit or stand to mirror the person you're speaking with. This is designed to put the other person at ease so you can quickly reestablish rapport. For example, if the other person leans in, lean in yourself. Watch gestures, stances, and where people put their hands, and subtly mirror them.

Scientists find that people perceive others who mirror their actions as being friendlier and more competent than people who don't. (Researchers call this the *chameleon effect*.) Highly effective salespeople often use body language mirroring, whether consciously or not.

You may find that you're already mirroring people without realizing it. Adjusting the angle of an arm or foot, or tilting the head, might be enough to complete the effect.

MIRROR AND NOTICE

Ask a friend or trusted colleague to join you for an experiment. Have the person tell you about a recent vacation or business trip. As the other person speaks, first try body mirroring without communicating what you're doing. Notice that you can do this without detracting your attention from the conversation or drawing the person's notice.

Then change your stance mid-conversation. Lean in and see if the other person mirrors you. Lean back or cross your arms, and observe if that changes the course of the conversation. Does the conversation falter or stall?

When you're done, ask the other person about the conversation. Which part made him most comfortable? Did he notice a shift? Notice how you felt about it. Do you feel that you developed a better rapport with the person when you were mirroring him?

You may be surprised by the extent of the role of body language in conversation.

ECHO WORDS TO CREATE RESONANCE

When you speak with people using their own words, they sense that they have been heard. Your questions and observations resonate deeply, traversing neural pathways they have already created.

As simple as this strategy sounds, it's quite rare in business.

When listening to others, we usually translate what we hear into our own favorite words. When taking notes, we write down our opinions or filter what's being said. We ask questions from our own viewpoint. We may believe we appear intelligent by rephrasing what was said in a different context. We delight in exercising our own vocabulary, perhaps including industry jargon.

But if you really want someone to think you're brilliant, use that person's same words in your responses.

Change your note-taking habits to focus on the precise words that others use. Listen for words that have "juice" or energy behind them.

For example, imagine you hear the following from a team member: "We did not hit our target for last quarter, which was 250 million. We fell short by 10 million. However, that was well within the range of seasonal variability. I think it's close enough, and doesn't threaten our ability to hit the year-end goal."

To practice echoing key words, your notes might look like this:

- Did not hit our target

- Fell short by 10 million

- Seasonable variability

- Within range

- Close enough

- Year-end goal

When you respond, frame any comments and questions using those same key words. For example,

"You say that we fell short by 10 million this quarter. Does the board know that we're close enough to meet the year-end goal?"

"Can you add background data on the seasonable variability to the board presentation, so they can see why we believe we'll hit our target?"

You're not parroting back everything the person said. Instead, you're using the most important words and phrases to promote a productive discussion to demonstrate that you're really listening. The speaker immediately understands what you're asking and feels that you're taking her side.

CONNECT THE PERSONAL STORIES

We are all the heroes of our own internal stories. Another way to build rapport with people is to find places where your story intersects with another's outside of the current context.

Possible points of connection include friends in common, shared interests or hobbies, similar hometowns or alma maters, or having children of similar ages. Look for anything that demonstrates a common experience.

In today's online and networked world, it's easy to discover points of connection before you even meet someone. Quick research on LinkedIn and Facebook offers a wealth of insight. If a colleague offers to introduce you to someone, ask for more information about the person beforehand. What is she passionate about? What is unique about her? (Don't cross the line into digital stalking; make sure the personal connections are public and appropriate.)

When you start the conversation, take some time to explore the connections you share. Practice the small talk that builds rapport.

Small talk? In a book about moonshots and visionary leadership, why are we writing about small talk? Establishing rapport accelerates trusting relationships, and reinforces your leadership. Done well, small talk delivers big results.

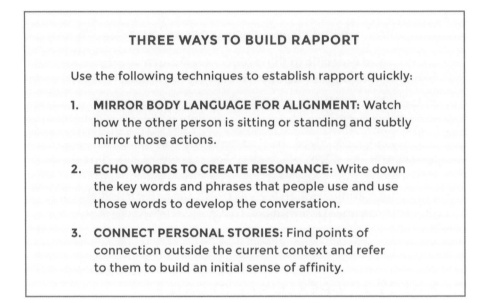

THREE WAYS TO BUILD RAPPORT

Use the following techniques to establish rapport quickly:

1. **MIRROR BODY LANGUAGE FOR ALIGNMENT:** Watch how the other person is sitting or standing and subtly mirror those actions.

2. **ECHO WORDS TO CREATE RESONANCE:** Write down the key words and phrases that people use and use those words to develop the conversation.

3. **CONNECT PERSONAL STORIES:** Find points of connection outside the current context and refer to them to build an initial sense of affinity.

WHEN RAPPORT IS CRITICAL

Unless you work entirely on your own, you won't get much done in business without establishing rapport with others. In some special situations, a minor investment of effort can generate a major payback.

Use mirroring in negotiations: Research shows that people who use "strategic mimicry" (mirroring body language) in negotiations get better results not only for themselves but also for those they negotiate with.

Echo key words when working across organizational boundaries: Moonshots require people to work across groups and step outside their usual haunts. The echoing technique highlights the words, phrases, and viewpoints that are core to the different teams. When you use their established words, you sound like an insider rather than an outsider, lowering barriers to effective discussion.

Use narratives in difficult conversations: Begin a challenging discussion by reconnecting the rapport you have established with small talk and personal stories to find commonalities.

THE SURPRISING SIDE EFFECT OF GOOD RAPPORT

Using these techniques may sound manipulative. And they *are*, but the person you're manipulating may be yourself.

Each of these techniques requires empathetic behavior, tuning you into the other person.

- Effective mirroring behavior requires that you closely observe the person you are speaking with, being truly present in the conversation.

- To echo key words, you have to listen carefully and put aside your own vocabulary and viewpoint to speak in the words of others.

- Connecting personal stories requires you to think about the other person's experiences. By doing so, you inevitably broaden your own perspective.

In the research into mirroring in negotiations, the individuals who used body mirroring negotiated better results *for everyone*, not just themselves. By aligning their bodies with their negotiation counterparts, the study participants also aligned their interests.

When you intentionally build rapport using these techniques, you will shape the way people perceive you. The greater benefit, however, may be that you become more insightful.

EXPAND YOUR IMPACT

Intentional Networking

I n the NASA biography of James Webb, one glimpses an individual who knew how to build and maintain his network. He was exceedingly busy while serving as NASA's administrator during the critical years from 1961 to 1968. But he recognized that the success of the mission depended, in part, on the strength of his personal and professional networks.

> 66 Through a variety of methods Administrator Webb built a seamless web of political liaisons that brought continued support for and resources to accomplish the Apollo Moon landing on the schedule President Kennedy had announced. 99
>
> NASA HISTORY OFFICE

When you're focused on meeting the next milestone, or buried in meetings and e-mails, networking often moves to the bottom of your to-do list. That's only natural. You don't have time to connect with colleagues or cultivate connections. You're engaged in more important and urgent tasks, right?

Because bold leaders operate outside of the context of business as usual, they understand how important it is to cultivate connections with people and perspectives beyond their own. To break through business as usual, expand your network.

Cultivating new contacts is important at *any* stage of a career. When you're engaged a moonshot, your business network may hold the key to overcoming breakdowns and discovering breakthroughs.

The demands on your time require you to be disciplined and strategic about cultivating connections. Like many of the other topics in this book, effective networking is a practice that you can establish and follow intentionally, for remarkable results.

Great leaders cultivate great networks.

THE DISCIPLINED NETWORKER

Perhaps you consider networking as a necessary evil of doing business, or something that happens naturally along the course of your career. But consider this: the people who benefit most from personal networks develop and maintain relationships intentionally.

Treat networking like the critical, ongoing business project that it is; manage and oversee it with discipline.

1. Dedicate a certain amount of time each week or month to developing connections. It doesn't take long to maintain your network. Networking pros dedicate 15–30 minutes a day; many do it first thing in the day so it's sure to happen.

2. Identify a target number of outreaches that you can make in that time window. Your goals might include:

    •   Number of outreach contacts per week/month

- Number of reconnections/contributions to existing contacts per week/month

3. Create and maintain a targeted list of people to connect with and relationships to maintain or cultivate in order to focus your limited time for the greatest impact.

When prioritizing outreach activities, use the following strategies: *reach across* domains and *level up*. Get to know people outside your usual circles.

Networking isn't about connecting with people to exploit their value. When you reach out with the genuine intention of building relationships, it brings significant benefit to you and to the person you're connecting with.

REACH ACROSS DOMAINS

Most people's professional networks are filled with individuals similar to them, occupying comparable roles in the same industry or working at the same companies. These networks happen naturally, without intentional effort.

Business networks gain value when they connect people *across domains*. Ideally, you will cultivate connections apart from the ones that everyone around you shares. Maintaining a broad network gives you the ability to connect people with others they do not know, and to draw on perspectives different than your own.

James Webb was a longtime Washington insider who cultivated a wide network as he lobbied for support for NASA in Congress and secured resources for the Apollo mission. The relationships he developed proved invaluable after the Apollo 1 accident in 1967. Webb took responsibility for the tragedy himself; on behalf of NASA, he got Congress to agree to allow his team to investigate the accident. With his strong network, Webb managed to deflect some of the backlash away from both NASA and the Johnson Administration and prevent damage to NASA's image and popular support.

Intentionally cultivate the breadth of your network. As you create your list, make sure you have people on it outside your current domain:

- People in different companies

- Leaders in other industries

- Others in different functional areas

Reach out to friends of friends. Research shows that these "weak ties," or friends of friends, are often rich sources of business advice, connections, and even job referrals.

LEVEL UP IN YOUR NETWORK

When you consider your networking prospects, include people with greater influence and scope than you. Connecting with influencers is a quick way to increase the impact of your efforts.

In his book *Business Brilliant*, Lewis Schiff suggests that networking skills were essential to the successes of Bill Gates and Guy LaLiberté (the latter is the founder of Cirque du Soleil). Schiff writes, "What set them apart was how they reached out and made networking inroads into somewhat alien worlds of superior wealth and resources."

Gates set out to build partnerships with the strongest computer industry players. Early on, he developed a relationship with IBM that secured his company's future. This relationship gave Microsoft the leg up on other competitors that shunned the traditional players and in doing so, lost the competitive edge because they failed to establish a partnership with an industry giant.

LaLiberté led the planning of Quebec's 450th anniversary celebration, and in doing so built connections with the city's government officials during Cirque's first summer. He leveraged the relationships he developed to extend his one-year project by convincing government officials to underwrite a second season of shows.

REACH OUT: MAKE IT EASY TO SAY YES

For most people, the hard part of networking isn't planning but *doing.* Many people don't feel comfortable "networking." You may have unpleasant memories of meeting with people who were hunting for favors or jobs or leads of one kind or another.

That's not how you're going to network.

Cultivate your network when you don't have a specific favor to ask, aside from learning or gaining insight. Focus on building relationships, not indebtedness. Do not ask for favors or create an expectation of obligation. Most people are flattered when you ask their opinion or acknowledge their expertise.

When you contact someone, make your intentions specific and clear, and include the three elements of effective outreach:

- Be specific about the time or interaction you're requesting. For example, ask for a 10-minute phone call or offer to buy someone a cup of coffee. Make a low-risk request that is easy for the other person to accept.

- Recognize the reason you've chosen to reach out to that particular person. Is the person an expert in an area you're interested in learning about? See the chapter on Acknowledgment for tips on tapping into the power of authentic acknowledgment.

- Either ask for advice or offer useful assistance.

If you're asking for advice, make the request low-risk and specific. Don't ask to "pick someone's brain." Don't ask for free consulting or a big commitment like mentorship. Start by asking for someone's quick reaction or thoughts on a specific topic. If possible, frame your requests as advice for others in your situation, rather than yourself personally.

- "Sam told me that you're an expert in the security industry and thought you might have opinions on how startups can best approach incumbents. Do you have 10 minutes to talk on the phone?"

- "I enjoyed the article you wrote for *Entrepreneur* magazine and am interested in how you think the strategies you outlined would apply to an established company. Can I buy you a cup of coffee?"

Networking in this way requires an investment of time. Learn about the person you're contacting to make an intelligent request or offer of assistance. Spend the time in the conversation, listening carefully and deeply. That's why you want to use these efforts strategically, intentionally developing the network that will support the moonshot and your career in the future.

Once you are with the person, ask great questions. Prepare in advance, but also look for ways to observe and respond to what you see. Meaningful conversations and interesting stories often arise from the questions that aren't prepped ahead of time.

- If you're meeting in the person's work environment, ask a question about anything unusual or interesting, from the cars in the parking lot to the artwork on the walls.

- Phrase your question in the context of something relevant and timely to the current day or situation. "What did you think about the announcement from Amazon today—does it signal a trend for the industry?"

- Notice and ask for more detail: "You mentioned the impact of cloud computing on this field. Tell me more about that."

CONTRIBUTE

Networking isn't easy, particularly when you're reaching out to those above you. It's tempting to operate within your own circles. Get over the discomfort of networking up by offering to contribute in some way. Your offer of a contribution may happen in the initial outreach or in the first conversation.

Have you ever had someone you barely know ask you, "How can I help you?" It's difficult to know how to answer that. You don't know what might be an appropriate scope, nor what the other person might be able to do for you, so you inevitably decline. Lesson: Don't make vague offers of assistance that are hard to act on.

Instead, offer something specific, even if it's small:

- "I love what you're doing with this program. Can I put you in touch with anyone at Acme?"

- "I just read a great article about a startup strategy that's relevant to our discussion. May I forward it to you?"

The offer might be as simple as recommendation of a favorite restaurant, if that's what you've been discussing.

Better yet, honor the advice the other person has given you by offering to pay it forward to others. For example, "I'm mentoring women in the tech industry and am going to share these thoughts with them."

AVOID THE UNSPECIFIC OFFER

"How can I help you?"

Those simple words can turn a first conversation into an uncomfortable, awkward encounter. When you request a meeting with someone and make this vague offer, it can work against you in many ways.

First, the other person probably doesn't know how you could help him, or what an appropriate request would be, and will decline.

Second, it suggests that you're thinking of his spending time with you as a transaction, which diminishes his generosity.

Finally, asking this question presumes that you're in a position to help the other person, which may alter the social structure of the interaction. This can be a problem if the person showed up to support you.

Be specific in any offers of assistance, and be transparent when asking for support.

ACTIVATE AND MAINTAIN THE NETWORK

Once you've built the network, use it. Reach out and ask for advice about breakdowns or insight into opportunities. Actively contribute to others, providing relevant articles or useful introductions.

- A large and broad network serves as an invaluable source of advice and experience, expanding your perspective.

- Asking for advice strengthens connections. The request gives someone an opportunity to contribute and increases personal investment in your success.

- Making occasional contributions creates a sense of goodwill and shared objectives with others, while keeping positive interactions in recent memory.

When seeking advice or perspectives, consider reaching out to friends of friends or people in different areas. They may provide insight that is far removed from your current perspectives. To find these ties, ask your network for referrals:

- Who else do you know who has experience in a sharing economy startup?

- Who do you think I should talk to about opening an office in the Boston area?

At Nokia, when the "big idea" team was within two days of its presentation to executive staff, they realized they had not yet validated the concept with the target audience: heavy mobile phone users in the 18–24-year-old demographic. One of the team members had a relationship with a business school professor at nearby Columbia University. The team asked him if they could invite a few students to visit their office to see a prototype of their product concept. They offered the students train fare and lunch. The team expected only a handful of students to take them up on the offer. The next day almost two dozen college students showed up at the Nokia office in New York. The team had to scramble to bring in more lunches and find a larger meeting room.

The team showed the students mock-ups and screenshots, and video-taped them using the prototype. The students stayed for more than four hours, excited to share their ideas and feedback.

As a result of the session, the team made a couple of critical last-minute changes to the prototype and included video clips of the college students in their presentation. They later learned that the video clips were essential to validate the product concept, and proved critical to securing support and funding for the project.

When you seek advice, use the opportunity to connect with people you have not contacted in a while—dormant connections from your past. If their careers have diverged from your own, they may have broader insights while still understanding your perspective.

Don't think of a network as a bank account from which you make regular withdrawals, or a ledger-based accounting of favors granted and claimed. Taking this approach shuts down the possibilities for serendipity and generosity.

Instead, look for ways to contribute to others in a manner that does not exceed your available time and resources for networking. Regular contributions are part of your intentional networking discipline.

For example, make a practice of fulfilling "five-minute favors" or things you can do for others in five minutes or less. Watch for articles of interest you can send to those in your network. Invite others to interesting events. Find opportunities to provide something of value to connections.

When you contribute freely to others, you expand the set of people who are willing to engage in your success. Having a strong network gives you access to resources that make you a better leader.

BE A HERO-MAKER, NOT A HERO

Recognize and Inspire Heroic Action

Successfully completing a moonshot requires heroic effort from many people. The first astronauts were heroes and public figures. The Apollo 11 mission carried television cameras onboard and broadcast images, both of Earth from space and of the astronauts.

People want heroes.

According to astronaut Eugene Cernan:

> *Along the way, and totally unexpected by us, we astronauts became very visible public figures. This wasn't NASA's initial intent, but they adapted quickly. It was the press, and in turn the public, who declared us heroes.*

Great leaders elevate the performance of those around them, inspiring and supporting team members and group collaboration. When these leaders engage on moonshots, heroes emerge around them.

> *Not every great leader is a hero-maker,*
> *but nearly every hero-maker is a great leader.*

Neil Vogel, the CEO of About.com, recognizes the value of elevating those around him. "The leader of an organization should definitely not be the hero. When there is success, the leader gets all the credit anyway," says Vogel. "Elevating other people as heroes is much better for the organization. When the CEO empowers other people to lead and demonstrates faith in them, the rest of the organization will too."

To become a hero-maker, you must abandon the role of the hero for yourself and cultivate the heroic in those around you. We're not suggesting that you forgo publicity for your efforts. Rather, give those on your team opportunities for visibility and growth, which sometimes means giving up personal recognition. Let the team present its findings to the executive committee. When seeking praise and recognition, advocate for your team and specific contributors rather than yourself.

As a leader, you gain recognition through your success in supporting the business and those who work with you.

> *Hero-makers acknowledge and inspire heroic effort.*

The first step on the path to being a hero-maker is to abandon the personal insistence on being *right*.

AM I RIGHT OR AM I RIGHT?

Every time you interact with your team members, you face an essential choice: Do I want to be *right*, or do I want to be *effective*? Ask yourself that question ahead of every conversation and meeting. It will change the way that you interact with others.

This simple idea can be difficult to internalize and practice, so repeat it to yourself:

I can strive to be right or to be effective—not both.

Proving yourself right keeps your focus firmly on your own position and interests. Even if you're confident you know what's right for the company, defending that position presents several risks to leadership:

- It closes the door to creative suggestions from the team, and sends the message that their contributions are not valued.

- Insisting on your own correctness makes you less open to hearing other opinions. What if others know something you do not?

- A defensive posture distracts the focus from where it really belongs, which is the broader business or customer interests.

If you succeed in pressing your point about a specific issue, you almost always fail in the leadership role.

A leader's job is to elevate the contributions of the entire team. Leaders cannot make heroes of those around them, or even encourage growth on the team, while insisting on being right all the time.

The best teachers understand that their job isn't to teach students facts, but to teach them to learn and think critically. This type of instruction takes more time and effort up front, but the long-term payoff is enormous.

Of course there are times as a leader when you need to assert your position despite opposition. But even then you don't need to insist on being right. Instead, you can acknowledge the validity of the other position, agree to disagree, and let others know that ultimately it's your call. When you demonstrate respect for their opinion and process, they're more likely to contribute their ideas and opinions in the future.

Is your job to solve a problem or to build a successful and enduring business? In leadership roles, it's usually the second.

FIND YOUR GAME CHANGERS

In the game of soccer (football in most of the world), substitutes play a critical role in long, grueling contests. When coaching the US Women's Soccer team in the 2015 World Cup, Jill Ellis kept essential players on the bench for certain games and changed her starting roster during the course of the tournament. She called her substitute players *game changers*, and they were. Words matter; this label presents every player with the opportunity to step into a heroic role.

Ellis's game-changer strategy paid off a few hours before the team's quarterfinal match against China when her two star players, Megan Rapinoe and Lauren Holiday, were suspended because of yellow card accumulation. Until that moment, Ellis's plan for this game did not involve changing the lineup. But now a lineup change was necessary. Ellis inserted midfielders Morgan Brian and Kelley O'Hara into the starting lineup, and started Amy Rodriguez at forward in place of Abby Wambach, allowing Carli Lloyd to defend less and attack more.

Lloyd scored a header that won the quarterfinal game 1-0. The changes elevated Lloyd's performance and created new sparks of connections between players. "Pushing me a bit higher enabled me to play free," Lloyd said. "I no longer thought about making mistakes and holding back on defense; I just went for it."

FROM *RIGHT TO EFFECTIVE* WITH AN APOLOGY

If you have already established a pattern of having all the answers and telling those around what and how to think, changing course will require a change in your relationships. The fastest path to repairing team relationships is an apology.

Don't apologize for your opinions. Instead, apologize for *not hearing* others. For example:

"When you presented your option, I was so set on my own approach that I did not hear you out. I apologize for that."

An apology exhibits vulnerability, which shifts the relationship and creates a foundation for trust. It clears the path for a real discussion. Having apologized, continue to ask yourself, "Am I insisting on being right?"

THE ONE-WEEK PROBLEM-SOLVING CLEANSE

If you have built your career by solving problems for others, changing your leadership style will require behavior changes from both you and your team. People now expect you to solve problems and provide answers. This robs them of the opportunity to demonstrate heroism.

Try this to reset your leadership style. For one week, commit to *not* solving any problems that people bring to you. Banish assertions from your vocabulary and only ask questions instead.

If someone comes to you with a problem, query the person in depth. The first question may be "What do you recommend?" If the person you're talking with doesn't have a recommendation, guide the conversation using questions that reveal a viable course of action:

- "What will it take to get this project back on schedule?"

- "What impact will this have on our overall deadline? Who else knows about this situation?"

- "Have you talked with R&D about alternatives?"

Limit your discussion to asking questions. Let team members take responsibility for making recommendations and solving problems. You'll learn that as a leader, you don't need to be the best problem solver. Instead, you develop excellence when you support others to solve problems independently.

Many executives find this exercise difficult. They rise through the ranks and gain recognition by being decisive and solving problems. But after a few days, people start to show up differently, presenting problems clearly and thinking through viable solutions on their own. This simple exercise transforms teams, creates new leaders, and elevates the heroes around you.

PART THREE

High-Performing Teams

The success of a moonshot hinges on choosing a courageous team. Team members have to be willing to engage in something that has never been done before, to step outside of their customary roles and inspire each other. Moonshots transform groups into tightly knit, high-performing teams. Undertaking a moonshot is a major challenge for a team.

In working with teams pursuing moonshots, we've identified eight critical success factors that make the largest impact on team performance. The chapters in this section outline those practices and can guide teams in the transition from business-as-usual behavior to high-functioning performance. While practices apply in any business setting, we've found them particularly important to fueling a moonshot:

- **THE FLIGHT PATH:** Map the milestones

- **CULTIVATE A HIGH-PERFORMING TEAM:** Mission rules and crew conduct

- **MEETINGS THAT DRIVE ACTION:** The secrets of high-performance meetings

- **TEAM COMMUNICATIONS:** I read you loud and clear

- **THE ART OF REQUESTS:** From intention to words to action

- **COMPLETIONS AND LANDINGS:** Celebrate success and maintain momentum

- **DIFFICULT CONVERSATIONS:** Communicate with clarity and compassion

- **FROM BREAKDOWN TO BREAKTHROUGH:** How to resolve problems

THE FLIGHT PATH

Map the Milestones

66 It may turn out that [the space program's] most valuable spin-off of all will be human rather than technological: better knowledge of how to plan, coordinate, and monitor the multitudinous and varied activities of the organizations required to accomplish great social undertakings. 99

SCIENCE MAGAZINE,
November 1968

To handle the enormity of the lunar landing challenge, NASA pioneered the principles and practices of modern project management. They created systems for coordinating communications among various groups, and charted the path to the moon by working backward from the end-of-the-decade deadline.

To manage the complexity, the NASA team developed a series of phases and steps with go/no-go decisions. Milestones included putting a man in orbit, sustaining a manned flight long enough to make the journey and return, simulating a lunar landing, etc. The planners knew that they could only discover what they needed to learn by taking action. Despite the unknowns, they broke the task into attainable steps, created plans and milestones, and got to work.

Complex, multi-function projects often rely on project management tools and practices. Even the best of these plans don't always maintain a sufficient level of urgency and focus throughout the project. It's not enough to be *busy*; activity is secondary to the results achieved along the way.

High-performing teams value results over activity,
and know the difference between the two.

Teams that elevate performance beyond the ordinary and execute a moonshot maintain urgency and stay focused on results. These are five practices that contribute to long-term success:

1. Define milestones in the currency of the end result

2. Create frequent project checkpoints

3. Identify critical go/no-go milestones

4. Jump-start momentum with quick wins

5. Leverage the magic of a compressed timeline

DEFINE MILESTONES IN THE CURRENCY OF THE END RESULT

What would you do if you wanted to run a marathon? You might work with a coach to plan a strategy for the race. The race has a clear starting line and time, and a defined finish line. Along the way, mile markers show you how far you have come, and the distance remaining.

If you understand your strategy, you can use milestones to instantly assess whether you are ahead of, at, or behind your plan. You certainly wouldn't measure your progress based solely on how many strides you've taken or how you're feeling. Your legs may feel great or they may ache. You may be winded or feel strong. But those factors don't affect *where you are* at a specific point in time relative to where you want to be. You are either running to your plan or you are not.

A moonshot is like a marathon; your objective is to create a strategy or road map that offers instant insight into whether or not you are on plan to meet your goal.

Too often, teams set off on ambitious projects without doing the work to define useful interim milestones. Those markers offer essential insight into where you are in your plan, and enable data-driven decisions.

> *The most effective teams use data, not opinions,*
> *to determine whether the project is on track or off track.*

An effective milestone is based on *results* and focuses on the *what*, not the *how*, of progress. The most effective milestones are expressed in the same measurements as the end result. When running a 10K race, for example, measure your progress in kilometers, not miles.

> *Define project milestones in the currency*
> *of the outcome.*

GE leaders knew that the "Ecomagination" initiative had to be more than a feel-good plan, so they set clearly defined milestone targets to drive execution. Objectives included investing $700 million R&D in clean technology by 2010, doubling revenues from the "Ecomagination" products, and reducing greenhouse gas and water usage. Specific metrics quantified the initiative's threefold objectives of spurring innovation, increasing revenues, and reducing the company's environmental footprint. These targets made the initiative real; they also inspired engineers to solve complex, global puzzles in order to meet their targets.

The number of milestones varies according to the length and the critical nature of the project. Milestones don't have to be evenly spaced. Making progress often requires a great deal of up-front planning and research.

As projects continue, it's difficult to maintain urgency and focus. Moonshots benefit when teams devote the same energy and urgency in the middle and at the end of the endeavor as they do at the start. The team may choose to insert more project milestones in the middle and end and to increase the frequency of check-ins.

The leader's job is to track progress on that plan, and to manage and resolve the inevitable deviations from plan as they arise.

CREATE FREQUENT CHECKPOINTS

Sales teams have quarterly quotas, and sales activity heats up in the last weeks and days of a quarter. Checkpoints create motivation. When you schedule checkpoints to assess progress and renew commitment from team members, you sustain urgency and focus.

Even if you're on track, regular checkpoints may accelerate progress toward a milestone. They also create opportunities to identify breakdowns and deliver project breakthroughs. Consider establishing frequent check-points for moonshots, perhaps every 30 days, to assess progress.

At the start of a project and at each checkpoint, ask every member of the team these questions:

- What key results must be achieved by the next checkpoint to be on track for the project?

- What resources and support do you need to achieve your results and breakthroughs?

Ask someone on the team to record what each person commits to producing. At the next checkpoint meeting, after reporting on the status of the results and breakthroughs, ask the team to assess whether anything has changed that might affect the plan, timeline, or decision to move forward with the moonshot.

As an example, the team member responsible for monitoring the industry landscape for a mobile software company revealed at a 30-day checkpoint that a competitor had launched a product with features that would make their product under development less competitive. The team decided to modify the feature requirements to better address the threat, and to find a way to maintain the current timeline, as time-to-market had become even more urgent with the latest market entrant.

When companies fail to frequently assess whether or not to move forward with a project, they end up with legacy initiatives without clear benefit to the company. This is especially important given the rapid pace of technological innovation. We rarely ask ourselves, "What can we *stop* doing?"

Implementing 30-day checkpoints establishes a foundation for an agile corporate culture that adjusts its course as needed.

IDENTIFY CRITICAL GO/NO-GO MILESTONES

Moonshots of a long duration benefit from a special kind of milestone: go/no-go milestones.

NASA used the go/no-go terminology for launch status checks. At critical points in the mission, such as immediately before liftoff, directors surveyed flight controllers. Each reported whether their specific area was still on course for launch. Go/no-go milestones are those milestones that are essential for the project to proceed.

Reporting "go" is a way of green-lighting the continuation of the project. Reporting no-go identifies an issue that must be resolved before the project can move ahead. In some cases, no-go decisions are critical enough to shut down or force a complete reassessment of a project. Ideally, the team establishes the criteria for go/no-go at the beginning of the project.

Of course "go" reporting does not always prevent problems. In the case of the Moonshot, the Apollo 3 accident was the result of an oxygen tank failure that shut down critical fuel cells. The Apollo Accident Review Board determined that the failure was caused by an unlikely chain of events and could not have been predicted.

JUMP-START MOMENTUM WITH QUICK WINS

Getting started on a moonshot can seem overwhelming. Difficult, complex projects often flounder due to "paralysis by analysis" and the pull of everyday pressures. One way to overcome inertia is to ask team members to commit to a quick win.

To launch a moonshot with momentum, install quick wins at the project's initial launch meeting. Ask everyone to write down one action they will take that will have a major impact in a short time frame. The deadline is the next time the group meets, ideally one or two weeks in the future and never more than 30 days out.

A senior executive team at a leading media and content publishing company initiated a project to restructure the company from an organization based on functions to business units. At the end of the project kick-off meeting, each executive identified a 30-day quick win that would add fuel to the project. These are a few of the quick wins the team members identified:

- Reorganize and reorient the product planning meetings around a vertical focus

- Scope the development work required to support channel rebranding

- Deliver one vertical industry story that the sales team can use

- Create framework for vertical General Manager compensation

- Deliver first-half Profit and Loss reports, segmented by vertical industry

As the executives committed to their quick wins, the CEO was overwhelmed by the individual pledges. He told the group that making these public and group-endorsed commitments was in itself a significant breakthrough for the project.

By sharing a quick-win pledge with the group, each team member commits to making a personal impact on the success of the project. Sharing these commitments reinforces personal accountability to the team. We find that as people step up to challenging and inspiring breakthroughs, they inspire each other.

Have someone on the team record and distribute the team's commitments within 24 hours of the meeting. The short time frame creates urgency, giving a boost to what might otherwise seem like a distant objective.

THE MAGIC OF A COMPRESSED TIMELINE

A tight time frame alone can transform a major objective into a moonshot.

The head of Human Resources at a large retail and manufacturing corporation learned that others in the business perceived the HR department as an unresponsive "black hole" in which e-mails and messages went unanswered for days or weeks. Determined to change that perception, she called her team together to explore solutions.

She challenged her team to a tight timeline: within 30 days, the team would commit to and achieve same-day response time to e-mails. Meeting this commitment would require a significant change in behavior, and in turn alter the way the department interacted with the rest of the organization.

The team implemented daily five-minute, stand-up meetings to track progress toward their goal. Each morning, team members recorded on a whiteboard the number of unresolved e-mails remaining from the previous day. As days passed, individuals drew encouragement from each other, sharing the practices that created their dramatic improvements in response time. By the 10th day, all but one person had managed to clear the backlog; the transformation had taken place faster than anyone anticipated.

What happened next illustrates how working together toward a tight timeline can transform teams. At the 10-day mark, the team decided as a group to gather around the one person who still had a backlog and work together to respond to every e-mail until the backlog was cleared. With the entire team engaged, this task took just an hour. The entire department had achieved the promised commitment to improving its service. The mini-moonshot had a huge cultural impact, transforming the group's interactions with the rest of the company and each other.

CULTIVATE A HIGH-PERFORMING TEAM

Mission Rules and Crew Conduct

The successful pursuit of a moonshot requires a combination of culture and people. When we invite people to participate in a moonshot, it immediately changes their lives. A moonshot challenges people to blast through their comfort zones to perform at higher levels.

It's easy to get the right people to jump on board with the concept of going to the moon.

Moonshots are exciting and entice people to participate.

When aligning a team around a moonshot, develop ground rules for working together. How will we make decisions? What "early warning systems" will we install to alert us to possible breakdowns? How responsive will we be to each other?

By tackling the ground rules first, teams elevate their expectations for working together; they also establish an explicit culture as a first result.

Use the following practices to break through the gravitational pull of ordinary teamwork and elevate teams to the highest levels of performance:

- Define the mission rules

- Assemble the right team

- Clear the decks

- Fire quickly and compassionately

DEFINE THE MISSION RULES

Teams develop unique cultures over time. As people work together, it simply happens. These unintentional team cultures often include practices that work well and others that don't. Distinguishing the two is critical.

One of the most common, unintentional cultural practices is being late for meetings. When people show up late for meetings, they telegraph several messages:

- Disrespect for other people's time

- The lack of effective personal organizational practices

- Lateness as an acceptable practice within the organization

- Lack of accountability within the culture

- Toleration of arrogance and self-importance

Lateness is not an intentional cultural practice, yet for many companies it becomes standard operating procedure.

In one company we work with, being late for a meeting is grounds for immediate firing. With this clear and unequivocal expectation, people never show up late; most arrive at least 10 minutes early. Employees report that the practice of showing up early delivers unexpected benefits: they feel more prepared and productive—and less stressed. People have started arriving early, and teams benefit by spending a few minutes together before the meeting begins.

Take a stand for being on time.
This sets a project and its leader apart.

Why wait for effective practices to evolve, or risk relying on unspoken rules? To operate at the highest levels of effectiveness, teams begin moonshots by agreeing on the team culture. Codify the team's operating procedures and expectations intentionally.

RULES OF ENGAGEMENT

Teams that develop and share their own code of conduct, with clear and explicit expectations, create the culture they want to inhabit.

When people write down and share Rules of Engagement, cultural expectations become *explicit*. The team culture does not always mirror corporate culture. High-performing teams have higher standards and different ways of operating.

The process of assembling and agreeing on internal team rules may also reveal individuals who do not fit the intentional culture or who are unwilling to change their way of working. When you intentionally define the team's culture you weed out those who don't have "The Right Stuff" for your moonshot.

SAMPLE RULES OF ENGAGEMENT AGREEMENT

**Here is an example of a Rules of Engagement used by
a leadership team at a global information technology company:**

1. I will take a clear stand for the possibilities and effectiveness of our strategic intent and will express that stance consistently to others.

2. I will actively acknowledge my/our accomplishments toward realizing the strategic intent.

3. I will reply to communications from other team members in the following response times:

    Voice: _____ hours   E-mail: _____ hours

4. I will be on time and prepared for any scheduled and accepted meetings, phone calls, or other agreed-upon commitments, and will acknowledge to team members any unfulfilled promises that I have made.

5. I will act appropriately to communicate or correct inadequate performance from myself or others, rather than overlook it.

6. I am willing to receive input in a direct and straightforward manner, and to offer input to colleagues and team members.

7. When I observe complaints, I will turn them into powerful requests for action and address the requests to someone who can act on them.

8. Where my work calls for the contribution of others, I will enlist their participation or respectfully allow them to decline and provide an alternative.

9. I will speak and act respectfully to everyone in the organization, recognizing that they are an extension of my network of assistance. I will not gossip or show a lack of respect to anyone in the organization.

10. I agree to responsibly resolve all issues and problems in my area of accountability within the framework of these agreements.

_____   _____
Signature of Team Member   Date

ASSEMBLE THE RIGHT TEAM

Moonshots require a special kind of team. Not everyone is cut out to be part of the initial team to lead a moonshot. Ideal types for the core moonshot crew include:

- Superstars: people who are known for consistently producing outstanding results

- Exceptional collaborators: strong team players known to bring out the best in those who work with them

- Risk takers: people who demonstrate problem solving and love to do things that have never been done before

- Wildly creative types: people who excel at innovation and ideation

- Results-oriented individuals: people who are known to own and drive initiatives, deliver on time, and make things happen

Moonshot leaders recruit the right talent from wherever it exists within or outside the company. Moonshot projects that we work with often round out internal teams with outside experts, collaborators, and contract resources.

CLEAR THE DECKS

The leader's job is to make it possible for the team members to participate—freeing time, attention, and focus so people can fully engage in the project. One of the best ways to break through business as usual is to take the team away from the business altogether.

This is especially critical for moonshots that launch in large, bureaucratic corporate environments—like the team on Nokia that worked on the MOSH project. Many of the moonshot leaders we serve relocate their teams to a different area of the office or a separate building.

Here are some things to consider when setting a team on the course for a moonshot:

- How do you offload team members' day-to-day responsibilities to others?

- How can you ensure the availability of funding and resources so the team can operate uninhibited?

- How can you protect the team from the bureaucratic practices that might otherwise stifle progress?

A check-in meeting during one moonshot project revealed that day-to-day responsibilities were impeding the team's ability to keep the project on track. The team decided that the only way to succeed was to "resign" from their day-to-day duties. They held an emergency meeting with the CEO during which all five team members placed their badges on the CEO's desk and declared their resignation from their usual roles.

The executive lead for the moonshot requested that the CEO work with her to reassign their previous duties to other members of the organization so the team members could focus 100 percent of their time on the moonshot.

During Epting's moonshot at Nokia, she needed to secure more time for Atte, a senior software developer working on an upcoming product release elsewhere in the company. The project had come to a standstill and required Atte to engage fully to move it forward. Epting was worried that Atte's manager wouldn't let him go because the project he was working on was at a critical point, just prior to release. Epting asked Atte's manager if they could find someone else who could substitute for Atte. To her surprise, he agreed. Together they identified several engineers who could serve as replacements. Epting and Atte's manager negotiated with other teams to transfer an engineer to replace Atte, and released Atte to rejoin their moonshot team. This act was a significant turning point in the project.

FIRE QUICKLY AND COMPASSIONATELY

Pursuing a moonshot may reveal people who are not suited to the task. The leader's responsibility is to put the needs of the team first and act swiftly and decisively to protect the integrity of the team.

Firing someone may be necessary, and it's one of the hardest things you'll have to do. Because letting someone go is so uncomfortable, people often delay making that decision, and instead try to compensate for a problematic employee long after it's apparent to everyone that the situation isn't working.

When people don't fit on a team, it's usually due to one of the following reasons:

1. They are not on board with the core objective or vision of the team.

2. They disrupt the team dynamic and effectiveness.

3. They cannot perform at the required level.

You owe it to the individual in question to make sure the person is in the right role and to determine if coaching can resolve the problems. Having done that, you owe it to yourself and the team to set the person on a different path. The hidden costs of keeping the wrong person on the team add up quickly.

Managing someone to compensate for a performance problem imposes a huge opportunity cost. When you spend disproportionately to manage a difficult or underperforming employee, it squanders time and energy, both of which are precious resources for a moonshot. Ask yourself:

•   What things could I be doing with the time and energy spent to manage a problem employee that would benefit the objective or the team?

•   Would I willingly pay an outside consultant to spend time managing that employee? If not, should I be spending *my* time on this effort?

Retaining a poor performer affects the team negatively. Others may resent working harder to compensate. Team members will question your leadership if you wait too long to terminate someone who obviously isn't working. All too often, they later ask, "What took you so long?"

Moonshots are especially sensitive to poor performance and require vigilance to ensure the team performs at its highest level. It's imperative for the leader to identify and redeploy those who fail to deliver or are not meeting the requirements of the assignment.

Don't fire someone lightly, but do act quickly. The longer a negative situation lingers, the greater its hidden costs.

THE DIFFICULT CONVERSATION

Few conversations are tougher than the one in which you let someone go. Approach it with the following internal guideline:

> *Fire someone in a manner that the person would want to work for you again.*

Be clear about the reason(s) you are taking action: lack of alignment with the core objective of the team, disruptive team dynamic or effectiveness, or failing to perform at the required level. The problem often appears to belong to all three areas, but we find that one of the reasons has primacy, and it's useful to know which one. Focus the conversation on the *external* reasons for the mismatch, not the attributes or traits of the person you're firing.

If the employee disrupts team dynamics, point to the Rules of Engagement. If it's a question of performance, discuss performance against outcomes and milestones. By focusing on objective facts, you avoid damaging the individual's dignity and sense of worth.

The most important thing to remember in this situation is to be kind and generous. You honor the employee, yourself, and the company with your compassion and integrity.

Questions to Ask When Considering Whether to Fire an Employee

- Given the team's current needs and what I now know, would I hire this person today?

- What is the cost to me personally of continuing to work with this person?

- What is the cost to the team? What resources are we spending to compensate for the individual?

MEETINGS THAT DRIVE ACTION

The Secrets of Effective Meetings

You can spot a high-performing team by how they manage meetings. Effective meetings have a clear objective established in advance. People understand their roles and contributions. Effective meetings are respectful of everyone's time and maintain momentum on vital projects.

High-performing teams run high-performing meetings.

Make your meetings more effective by following a few simple steps. The four components of an effective meeting are:

1. They start and end on time

2. They have an outcome-based purpose

3. They generate a list of committed actions (an action log)

4. They end with a powerful close

START *AND* END ON TIME

High-performing teams start meetings on time. Once you demonstrate that start times are real, people will show up on time.

Effective meetings also end on time.

For meetings longer than 15 minutes, we recommend that teams designate a timekeeper. The timekeeper creates a shared commitment from the group to keep the meeting on track.

MEETING PURPOSE

People call business-as-usual meetings for vague purposes, for example, to "discuss," "review," or "consider." In contrast, effective meetings have clear, outcome-based reasons for happening:

1. To resolve a problem

2. To make a decision

3. To brainstorm

ACTION LOG

An action log captures commitments made during the meeting, including the committed action, person who committed to it, and due date.

Actions define an explicit result. Make sure the person assigned the action understands the task and has agreed to the deadline. A single person, not a group, owns an action. The deadline is an explicit date and, often, time.

POWERFUL CLOSE

The end of a high-performing meeting is also what elevates it above business-as-usual practices.

One way to close a meeting powerfully is to ask all participants to state the one key thing they're taking away from the meeting. This reinforces what's important, keeps people focused, creates alignment, and ensures public commitment to outcomes.

MAINTAIN URGENCY WITH RAPID STATUS CHECK-INS

When working on a moonshot, frequent short meetings keep the project top of mind and maintain a sense of urgency.

For fast-moving, high-priority projects, daily five-minute stand-up meetings are particularly effective. In a stand-up gathering, have all team members report whether they are on track or if something has changed, and seek input from the group to make decisions or get approval.

The key to success is to keep these meetings to just five minutes. As a general rule for daily meetings, the longer the meeting, the less effective it becomes.

TEAM COMMUNICATIONS

I Read You Loud and Clear

Transcripts of the interactions between NASA flight controllers in Houston and the crews of the Apollo 11 program are a study in complete, clear, and effective communication.

Radio transmissions during the flights were sporadic and fragmented. Crews developed practices to ensure clear communications in even the worst of circumstances.

For the first lunar landing, NASA had selected the area of the moon they named Sea of Tranquility (Mare Tranquilitatis) because it is a relatively smooth and level place. In the last seconds before landing, Neil Armstrong discovered that despite its smooth appearance through a telescope, the Sea of Tranquility had a high density of craters. Armstrong had to manually pilot the lunar module landing to avoid a sharp-rimmed crater measuring some 180 meters across and 30 meters deep.

As a result of this detour, the lunar module was close to running out of fuel allocated for landing just 30 seconds before touchdown. Mission Control believed that if Armstrong ran out of fuel at a height of more than 10 feet, the touchdown would be harder than the landing gear was designed to withstand.

Here is a snippet of the communications between Armstrong from the lunar module, astronaut Buzz Aldrin from the Apollo 11 spacecraft, and Charles Duke from Mission Control during the final moments before the lunar module touched down on the surface of the moon.

> 102:45:31 DUKE: 30 seconds.
>
> 102:45:32 ALDRIN: Drifting forward just a little bit; that's good. (Garbled) (Pause)
>
> 102:45:40 ALDRIN: Contact Light. (At least one of the probes hanging from the lunar module footpads had touched the surface.)
>
> 102:45:43 ARMSTRONG (onboard): Shutdown (Armstrong had planned to shut down the engine as soon as the contact light came on.)
>
> 102:45:44 ALDRIN: Okay. Engine Stop.
>
> 102:45:45 ALDRIN: ACA out of Detent. (Attitude Control Assembly [ACA] was a control stick. Armstrong had put it on manual to pilot the lunar module.)
>
> 102:45:46 ARMSTRONG: Out of Detent. Auto.
>
> 102:45:47 ALDRIN: Mode Control, both Auto. Descent Engine Command Override, Off. Engine Arm, Off. 413 is in.
>
> 102:45:57 DUKE: We copy you down, Eagle.
>
> 102:45:58 ARMSTRONG (onboard): Engine arm is off. (Pause) (Now on voice-activated comm) Houston, Tranquility Base here. The Eagle has landed.

Similarly, moonshot teams become adept at communicating effectively and efficiently.

THE RULE OF THREE

Human beings are adept at recognizing patterns, and crave structure to make sense of things. Perhaps this is why information is often presented in groups of three.

Three is the smallest number of elements required to create a pattern. The pattern aids memory, while the number is small enough that it doesn't overwhelm us. The Rule of Three technique described below takes advantage of the seemingly magic properties of the number three. It's not just about paring down to three points—it's about picking the *right* three points.

The technique is useful any time you want to persuade someone, whether in a formal presentation, a meeting, or even an important conversation in support of your moonshot. It has—you guessed it—three guidelines, so it's easy to remember.

1. What is the desired *outcome* for this audience? What will you ask the audience to say or do as a result of the communication?

2. What three *beliefs* will promote that outcome? Note the specific wording: it's not about what you want to *tell* people, but what they need to *believe* in order for you to achieve your desired outcome. This question requires you to consider the other person's perspective.

3. What three key points, or supporting arguments, are necessary to create each belief?

Using this strategy focuses your effort on the most important information so you can present it in a way that people understand and remember.

For example, as a potential buyer for a distressed business, you may make an introductory call to the current owner with the aim of setting up a next meeting for a formal discussion of your proposal. To achieve this outcome, the current owner would need to believe:

-   You are a credible potential buyer

-   You have experience turning distressed businesses around

-   You are someone the owner can trust and respect, and would be easy to work with

RULE OF THREE STRUCTURE

1. What is the desired outcome? _____
   _____

2. What is the first belief your audience must hold in order to achieve that outcome? _____
   _____

   Three key points or arguments supporting that belief:

   Supporting point: _____

   Supporting point: _____

   Supporting point: _____

3. What is the second belief your audience must hold in order to achieve that outcome? _____
   _____

   Three key points or arguments supporting that belief:

   Supporting point: _____

   Supporting point: _____

   Supporting point: _____

4. What is the third belief your audience must hold to achieve that outcome? _____
   _____

   Three key points or arguments supporting that belief:

   Supporting point: _____

   Supporting point: _____

   Supporting point: _____

Summarize and make a powerful request.

PROBLEM-SOLUTION-RESULT

In the typical business environment, people often delay or avoid communicating problems when they arise or they sound an alarm without taking action to resolve the issue. There's a reason for this: in many environments, communicating problems can invite conflict and blame.

Problem-Solution-Result (or P-S-R) is a simple and effective formula to report problems promptly and offer solutions. Though it sounds obvious, it's rarely practiced. When you address problems in this way, you and your team will rise above the hum of business-as-usual.

Using P-S-R, you describe the problem, state the solution, and report or predict the result. If you have not yet come up with a solution, identify a proposed solution and the results you expect.

Let's see how this applies in the real world. Take the case of a development manager who reports that her team will miss an important deadline because of a technical problem. Using the P-S-R formula, she might report as follows:

PROBLEM: "A critical component part of the new product just failed in manufacturing testing, and we don't have a second source. This will cause a delay of at least two weeks in our product release."

SOLUTION: "We don't have a solution yet. But we've set up an emergency meeting with the manufacturer tomorrow at 2 p.m. We've also reached out to other vendors to see if they can manufacture or source this part."

RESULT: "By 6 p.m. tomorrow I will present three options and their impact on the budget and schedule, and the team's recommendation as to how to proceed."

ON-TRACK OR OFF-TRACK REPORTING

Meeting fatigue infects many companies, stealing valuable time. Status meetings are especially ineffective when people spend too much time reporting activities, and too little time reporting results, sometimes in an effort to inflate activity to compensate for a lack of results.

Status meetings can be a crutch
for teams to value activity over results.

Here are some examples of what a typical status meeting might sound like:

- "Things are going well."

- "We've just resolved a major issue, and we're really happy to have that one behind us."

- "We had a great meeting with the vendor and they'll get us new pricing tomorrow."

- "We just presented to a new client and they LOVE our product."

- "I've tried to get engineering to resolve this Priority 1 bug and they haven't done it yet. I called them three days ago and they haven't returned my call."

These statements provide little useful information about the project. None address the fundamental question of whether the project is on track or off track.

On-track or off-track reporting delivers a binary yes/no answer based solely on facts. You have either met your specific objective relative to the current milestone or you have not.

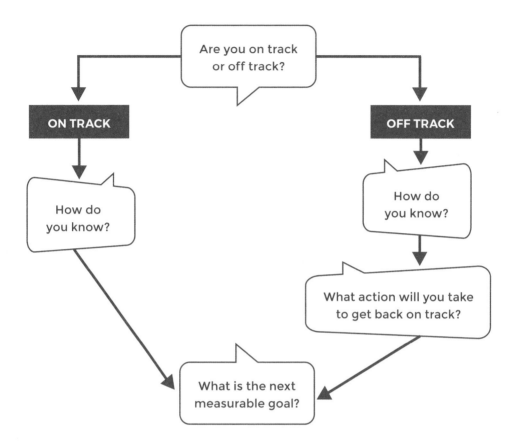

When leading a status meeting, ask your team to address only one question: Are you on track or off track? People tend to want to report on their activity, and many find it difficult to simply answer this simple question. Hold their feet to the fire with firmness and respect.

If, for example, the Sales Lead reports, "Oh, things are going great. I had a customer meeting this morning and the demo went really well."

A response to get an effective on-track or off-track report would be, "That's great. And you had promised last week to have secured three firm commitments from customers to participate in our beta program. Are you on track or off track for that goal?"

When they answer, the next question is, *how do you know?* Listen for fact-based evidence that corresponds to the key milestones in your project.

A fact-based answer might sound like this: "My goal was to have three customers commit to participating in our beta program. We are on track. As of today, we signed our third customer."

Then ask about the upcoming milestone: *What is the next measurable goal?*

If someone is on track, asking about the next milestone maintains the sense of urgency and brings up any potential problems. When someone is off track, create a plan *with a timeline* for getting back on track.

Here's how on-track or off-track reporting sounds:

The head of design says: "We are off track. Our milestone was to have completed wireframes by yesterday. We are two weeks behind. We worked out a new plan this morning that puts us back on track with only a week delay. Now we will deliver the new wireframes in three weeks. At that time we will have completed wireframes and in parallel we are moving ahead with design 10 of the landing pages, so we will be on track to complete the project on time."

To be effective, it's often useful to ask for more details about how team members know they're on track to make sure you don't miss anything.

THE ART OF
REQUESTS

From Intention to Words to Action

President Kennedy's speech to Congress in 1961, outlining the goal of landing a man on the moon, was an explicit request for a commitment and increased funding for the space program. This is what the president said immediately after declaring the moon as the objective:

> *Let it be clear—and this is a judgment which the Members of the Congress must finally make—let it be clear that I am asking the Congress and the country to accept a firm commitment to a new course of action, a course which will last for many years and carry very heavy costs: $531 million in fiscal '62—an estimated seven to $9 billion dollars additional over the next five years. If we are to go only half way, or reduce our sights in the face of difficulty, in my judgment it would be better not to go at all.*

The president explicitly asked Congress for commitment and money, on behalf of himself and the nation. Taken in the context of the speech, this was a well-formed request.

THE BUSINESS OF ASKING

A request turns words into action. High-performing teams operate on well-formed requests, while ineffective requests contribute to team dysfunction.

In a "command-and-control" work environment, leaders give orders and workers acknowledge them. But many work environments are non-hierarchical; they involve collaboration, autonomy, and distributed decision-making. Effective leaders no longer bark orders; they craft specific goals and make clear and well-formed requests.

A request isn't a command. By definition, the person receiving the request has the option of not accepting the request, or possibly making a counteroffer (for example, "I can do this by next Tuesday if I delay this other project I'm currently working on.").

Moonshots often require the contributions and cooperation of individuals across multiple departments or organizations, and the creativity and expertise of many. In pursuing a moonshot, people will ask for assistance and guidance from others on their teams and beyond. Achieving a moonshot requires us to master the art of making effective requests.

Effective requests successfully navigate several potential gaps, including the following:

- **COMMUNICATION GAP:** There's a gap between what you really want and how you ask for it. The gap results from using vague language about what you want, when you want it, or who will do it.

- **UNDERSTANDING GAP:** Requests often fail in the gap between the words you use and what the other person hears. Be explicit about expectations and deadlines in order to avoid surprises.

- **EXPECTATION GAP:** Another potential gap often exists between the expectations and commitments made between parties.

- **EXECUTION GAP:** Well-communicated requests can be sidetracked by other high-priority tasks. Initiatives can languish indefinitely between commitment and fulfillment. As the saying goes, the road to hell is paved with good intentions.

There's a formula to close the gaps and turn requests into action. It may not come naturally at first, but when you use it consistently, persistence pays off. Clear requests strengthen teams because they eliminate ambiguity, clarify commitments, and deliver results.

MAKE A COMPLETE AND CLEAR REQUEST

As simple as it may seem, requests often fail because they lack one of the following elements:

- A requestor and requestee

- Specific requirements

- A calendar-ready time frame

Requestor and Requestee

Have you ever heard "requests" like this?

- "This needs to be done."

- "Corporate wants to see the numbers."

- "It would be a good idea to . . ."

People often voice requests like this, then are surprised when nobody makes them happen. Why is there no action? Because these requests lack a requestor and a requestee.

Effective requests are made directly from one individual to another. Be explicit that you are making the request by saying: "I ask that you . . ."

or "Can you do this for me?" If you are asking on someone else's behalf, name the person.

It is equally important to be clear about exactly whom you are asking to take action. Requests fail when no one owns them.

An effective request with a legitimate requestor and requestee sounds like this: "Sue, I ask that you gather input from the team and write a two-page summary for me by next Wednesday at 5 p.m. Will you do that?"

Specific Requirements

Request a specific *outcome*, not a process. Requesting an outcome bridges the expectation gap, as the outcome is clearly defined. Focusing on the outcome has other benefits:

- This type of request demonstrates respect for the requestee's expertise and initiative. You request the *what*, and the person responding can determine *how* to deliver. You can offer suggestions if necessary.

- The requestee is accountable for a specific outcome rather than an ambiguous action or effort. When asked to research a price point, a person might search the web for 10 minutes and stop after finding nothing. But if you've asked for an e-mail with price details on the top three solutions in the market by 3 p.m. on Thursday, January 18, most people will dig until they can deliver the committed outcome.

When you are clear and specific with your requests, people are more likely to be clear and explicit with their commitments in response.

A Calendar-Ready Time Frame

Without a specific time frame, the chances of your request turning into action are unpredictable, subject to forces outside your control. Don't add this risk to your moonshot; create specific deadlines.

The time frame is a specific date, and may include the actual time of day. Using vague time frames like the following can doom a request:

- **"AS SOON AS POSSIBLE"**: This phrase leaves it to the requestee to determine the deadline and level of urgency.

- **"IN 30 DAYS"**: Starting from today? Would the end of next month work?

If you want results in a specific number of days, restate the time frame as a specific date. Instead of "in a week," say, "next Tuesday, the 12th." When you give a deadline a date, it goes into the calendar. Any conflicts or problems become apparent.

As a final note, psychologists have found that including a reason for a request increases compliance. If the reason for the request is clear, you might also add a reason for the deadline.

Putting this together may sound awkward at first. But when you are disciplined about using well-formed requests, you reap the benefits of faster, more consistent results.

TURNING THE ASK INTO ACTION

The ultimate goal of a request is to get commitment and action. To increase the odds of a positive outcome, establish the following:

- A clear, unambiguous response

- An agreed-upon follow-up

A Clear Response

When making a request, listen for the response and the commitment. Responses fall into one of three categories:

- Acceptance (yes)

- Counteroffer

- Denial or rejection

If the response is ambiguous, continue asking until you identify which of these three you hear. And beware the noncommittal yes:

If you see a nod or lack of explicit response, ask for a commitment: "George, you nodded your head. Does that mean you'll get me those numbers by Monday?"

If you get the noncommittal "That sounds like a good idea," don't mistake it for a "yes." Ask for a commitment.

You may get a counteroffer. For example, George might say, "I can deliver a list of vendors by Monday, as you asked, and the costs by the following Friday. Does that work?" In this case, negotiate until the counteroffer becomes a yes on both sides.

If the answer is no, clarify that fact right away. A clear rejection lets you move immediately to Plan B, which might entail reprioritizing projects or asking someone else. You might change the terms of the request, making a counteroffer of your own: "Can you give me the cost numbers for the largest vendor, Acme, by Monday?"

If you get a yes, identify and restate the commitment. Write the commitment in an action log or note it on your calendar so you can follow up to ensure it is completed on time.

Following Up

Without a follow-up, even the best-formed requests may fall into the execution gap and become buried by a pile of more urgent work.

Start the follow-up process as soon as you get a "yes" to your request. Ask if the requestee needs support to fulfill the request.

- "What resources do you need to make this happen?"

- "Is there anything you want from the team or me?"

Define exactly when and how you will check in, and schedule the follow-up in your calendar.

Clearly, every request doesn't merit this approach. Mission-critical requests warrant thoroughness and following up. Less critical requests may not require such formality.

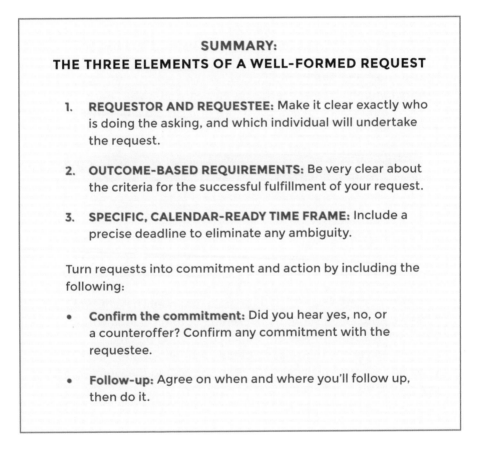

SUMMARY:
THE THREE ELEMENTS OF A WELL-FORMED REQUEST

1. **REQUESTOR AND REQUESTEE:** Make it clear exactly who is doing the asking, and which individual will undertake the request.

2. **OUTCOME-BASED REQUIREMENTS:** Be very clear about the criteria for the successful fulfillment of your request.

3. **SPECIFIC, CALENDAR-READY TIME FRAME:** Include a precise deadline to eliminate any ambiguity.

Turn requests into commitment and action by including the following:

- **Confirm the commitment:** Did you hear yes, no, or a counteroffer? Confirm any commitment with the requestee.

- **Follow-up:** Agree on when and where you'll follow up, then do it.

THE RED BINDER EFFECT

In a world where people track their lives on smartphones and cloud-based apps, many leaders we work with strengthen commitments for critical requests by recording them in a visible and tangible way.

Yes, we're talking about paper.

A CEO at a media company took extreme measures to address a chronic problem with her team's failure to meet milestones. She filled a red binder with pages containing empty columns to track requests and carried it with her to every meeting. The pages consisted of a simple chart that looked like this:

REQUEST	OF WHOM	BY WHEN

Her red binder served as a tangible reminder that she was tracking and taking seriously her team's commitments. Within a few weeks, the team was once again delivering on time.

You don't have to use a red binder. A bright-colored file or clipboard works equally well. Choose something that suits your style yet is visible and obvious to those around you.

COMPLETIONS AND LANDINGS

Celebrate Success and Build Momentum

The Apollo 11 Moonshot had two public landings: one on the moon and its triumphant return to Earth, courtesy of a splashdown in the Pacific Ocean. But there were dozens of liftoffs, landings, breakthroughs, and firsts in the years leading up to the 1969 lunar landing, including:

- The first Americans in orbit

- The first crewed spacecraft to change orbit

- The first crewed mission over seven days

- The first successful launch of a rocket capable of sending a crewed craft to the moon

- The first successful crewed orbit of the moon

Behind each milestone were countless technological and operational feats worth celebrating. The path to that momentous splashdown was rich with initiations and completions, successes and failures, all of which contributed to the final success of the project.

LANDINGS ARE MANDATORY

Greek mythology tells the story of King Sisyphus, whose deceitfulness angered the gods. As punishment, he was condemned to the unending task of rolling an enormous boulder up a steep hill. The boulder always rolled back down before reaching the top. His punishment was an eternity of futile, hopeless labor.

The modern-day parallel may be working on a team that pursues a major initiative with a moving finish line—perpetual "mission creep"— and few or no incremental milestones along the way. When teams stop to assess, celebrate, and reset, they learn from their efforts and recognize progress.

Endings create a meaningful narrative
and context for our work.

Completion points are essential in the pursuit of a moonshot. When you ask people to take on heroic efforts, they must be able to see the finish line and experience progress along the way. Without completion, burnout is inevitable.

A "completion" as defined here isn't about stopping. It's about marking the end of a phase, assessing what has happened, recognizing contributions, and moving onward. The longer the journey, the more segments, breakthroughs, and achievements there are to celebrate.

A completion point serves many purposes:

- Completions create opportunities to acknowledge progress and contributions.

- They offer a structure for reengaging and reaffirming commitment.

- Teams can use completion points to reflect on and learn from what has happened to date, correct course if needed, and elevate performance.

- Completions reset or redirect efforts, or bring closure to a phase of the project that might otherwise linger beyond its original due date.

- Completions provide teams with multiple, smaller wins that sustain motivation and maintain forward momentum and reduce the potential for burnout.

Completions are too valuable to save for the finish line. The best moonshots include many intentionally created landing points to mark, review, and celebrate progress.

WRITE YOUR OWN ENDINGS—LOTS OF THEM

66 If you want a happy ending, that depends, of course, on where you stop the story. 99

ORSON WELLES

Storytellers know that the ending shapes the story. Great leaders understand that where and how they mark completions creates the story arcs for their teams.

Completion is a creative act.

In your moonshot, consider marking and celebrating these five types of completions:

1. Milestones or Points in Time

The finish line and time-based milestones create natural points for marking completions. If key milestones have specific dates, amplify their impact by scheduling events to observe them in advance. Put them on the calendar to debrief and celebrate appropriately.

Match the scale of the completion event to the magnitude of the effort. A party is overkill for weekly milestones, but a call or note of acknowledgment may be appropriate.

When you complete a milestone, we recommend that the acknowledgment includes the following:

- Assessment of where you are relative to the ultimate goal

- Acknowledgment of the breakthroughs and heroic efforts that brought you to this point

- A quick discussion of the plan to reach the next milestone

Even if you didn't meet a milestone, recognize that fact and relaunch the effort toward a next milestone. If a major barrier blocks your progress, turn the milestone completion event into a problem-solving session. (See the chapter "From Breakdown to Breakthrough.")

If your milestones are few and far between, add markers for other calendar-based completion dates, such as end of year and end of quarter.

2. Breakthroughs or Heroic Efforts

Take the opportunity to acknowledge and celebrate the work when a team has experienced a breakthrough or completed a heroic effort.

For example, you might celebrate when the team:

- Reaches a major product milestone, such as a beta release

- Solves a particularly difficult technical challenge

- Launches a website

- Signs a partnership or other pivotal deal essential to the project

- Secures additional funding or resources for an initiative

- Hires key team members

- Gains positive customer validation

- Receives significant press or industry recognition

- Signs the first large customer

Many of the companies we work with ring bells when team members achieve critical milestones, such as closing a new deal. To stimulate risk taking and innovative thinking, another client gives out small acrylic "experiment awards" when an employee completes and reports the result of an experiment, regardless of whether it has a successful outcome.

Also acknowledge the personal breakthroughs that happen as part of a moonshot. If a team event isn't appropriate, take the individual to lunch or recognize their breakthrough at a meeting.

3. Completions Created Out of Thin Air

Sometimes a team engages on a long-haul project with no immediate end in sight. Good leaders recognize when spirits wane and find ways to install completions.

Bill, the president of the largest telecommunications company in the Midwest, was leading a yearlong project to reduce the company's churn rate. Four months into the project, Bill realized that every executive staff meeting was consumed by analyzing the churn numbers. The executives had become obsessed with churn and were neglecting critical issues in the business.

The project started with a single, monolithic goal: to drive the churn rate to less than 5 percent. Bill realized that by breaking the effort into smaller chunks, he could maintain momentum and enthusiasm for the project.

He called a company meeting and announced that the company had completed an invented "Phase One," which he called the "Design and Proof-of-Concept Phase." He enumerated the accomplishments and acknowledged the contributions of key team members. They celebrated the achievement of this invented milestone.

He then announced Phase Two, focusing on several key indicators that contributed to churn. This simple reframe of the project ignited creativity and participation at all levels, and injected the project with much-needed momentum.

4. Resets

What happens when you've missed a key milestone or are off-track to meet the next one? What if you have to abandon or modify milestones or otherwise face a breakdown on the path to your final goal?

Completion is an excellent way to stop, redirect, and reinitiate efforts to maintain or build enthusiasm for a project that is experiencing turbulence.

Transform a missed milestone into a reset by declaring, "That was Phase One, and it's behind us. Let's move on to Phase Two." Take the time to acknowledge and set a course to maintain motivation and demonstrate respect for the effort already expended.

Judicata, a startup developing a next-generation legal research solution, was driving toward a beta test release date for its product. The CEO, Itai Gurari, had established an ambitious goal for the beta release with targets to achieve six measures for near-perfect search engine accuracy.

Three weeks before the beta date it became clear that the development team was on track to hit four of the six targets, but unexpected complexity would delay solutions to the other two.

Rather than slip the whole release, Gurari called for all-hands meeting to discuss the situation. The team agreed to maintain the target beta date but lower the targets for the two difficult components. The team brainstormed how to achieve these goals, which were still very aggressive, and agreed to work late and over weekends to complete the work on time.

The team hit six goals on time. Gurari declared success and celebrated the team's extraordinary effort. Despite the near-miss on two of the targets, their work together was excellent and the team had gained a new level of confidence in their ability to tackle ambitious and difficult problems. As a result, morale surged and the team pulled together at a time when finger pointing may have otherwise torn them apart.

Teams that neglect the reset step may experience a lingering feeling of failure. When you initiate a "reset completion," include:

- What went well

- What you have learned

- How you will apply what you have learned

Create a different label for the past and the present, such as Phase One and Phase Two. Be sure to generate the completion criteria and milestone dates for what lies ahead. Reset completions give people a chance to reflect on and absorb lessons from the past while charting a clear path for progress.

5. Closures, Big and Small

Declaring a planning phase or decision cycle as complete signals people to move on. This strategy is particularly valuable when some people aren't ready to let go, such as a scientist who wants to keep exploring or an engineering team looking for perfection.

*Create a formal completion to give people
a mandate to move on.*

One CEO we know uses the strategy of calling completions very effectively in meetings and discussions. When a team works together to arrive at a solution through discussion, or when he makes a definitive decision about how to proceed, he will then ask, "OK, is that now complete?" When everyone agrees, the atmosphere shifts in the room. The issue goes from being under consideration to being done, and the discussion then moves on.

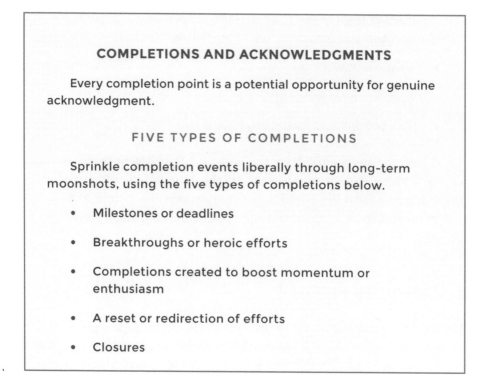

COMPLETIONS AND ACKNOWLEDGMENTS

Every completion point is a potential opportunity for genuine acknowledgment.

FIVE TYPES OF COMPLETIONS

Sprinkle completion events liberally through long-term moonshots, using the five types of completions below.

- Milestones or deadlines

- Breakthroughs or heroic efforts

- Completions created to boost momentum or enthusiasm

- A reset or redirection of efforts

- Closures

CAPTURING THE EFFECT

In the original *Star Trek* television series, the stories were theoretically pulled from the Captain's Log. Each episode described what had happened to the crew members in the course of that particular mission. Boldly go in search of the stories and the effects that accompany your moonshot.

During scheduled events to mark completions, ask team members and participants to reflect on and share examples of the changes they have noticed in themselves and others. Use the following questions to start people thinking in this direction:

- What changes have you noticed in the way that you work here since we started the moonshot?

- Has this project had a personal impact on you?

- Can you identify any breakthroughs that we have achieved since working on this?

- Have you noticed a significant shift in how you work with other team members?

- Has someone else on the team demonstrated new capabilities or strengths?

- What opportunities are now possible since undertaking this project?

The longer the journey, the more stories there are to capture and moments to celebrate. Completions are vital to the success of your moonshot. By marking completions you boost fuel reserves and keep the team motivated and on course.

DIFFICULT CONVERSATIONS

Communicate with Clarity and Compassion

Teams are defined and tested by how they handle adversity. Whether on a moonshot or not, managing team conflict entails difficult and uncomfortable conversations. How you approach these conversations affects team morale and effectiveness, and reveals the strength of your leadership.

Difficult conversations are those interactions that create anxiety or stress. In these conversations:

- The stakes are high

- Opinions conflict

- Emotions run strong

Negative emotions around difficult conversations cloud judgment and stifle creative solutions. When facing a difficult conversation, many of us fall back on old, familiar strategies that are ineffective and, in some cases, damage relationships and undermine our leadership.

Avoidance is one coping mechanism people use when faced with a tough interaction. Many employees avoid difficult conversations with managers or co-workers. Delays rarely improve the situation, as problems fester longer than necessary.

Another strategy is to barrel through the uncomfortable conversation quickly; deliver the news and then walk away. This approach leaves the other party in the conversation feeling unacknowledged and disrespected, more audience than participant. In a rushed conversation, participants have no opportunity to find points of agreement or shape each other's perception.

This strategy feels like a presidential press conference in which the president makes a statement and then walks away without taking questions. What happens next? Press speculation, 24-hour news cycles, and endless analyst spin. Consider this possibility: a similar news cycle may happen in the head of the other person. If the person discusses the conversation with friends and colleagues, the negativity can spin out of control.

Often the leaders we work with stress for days about delivering bad news to their team, only to find that the team already saw the news coming and was waiting for guidance and leadership.

Preparation is key to managing difficult conversations with clarity and compassion. Before any difficult conversation, follow these practices to prepare:

1. Unpack and identify the issues

2. Clarify your desired outcome

3. Shift perspectives

1. UNPACK AND IDENTIFY THE ISSUES

The first step in addressing a difficult conversation is to examine everything, separating the issues to determine how to act on each.

Once you clarify the issues, place each in one of three buckets:

- A request

- Information to communicate (delivering bad news)

- A problem to solve

With this insight, you can prepare the proper strategy for each issue.

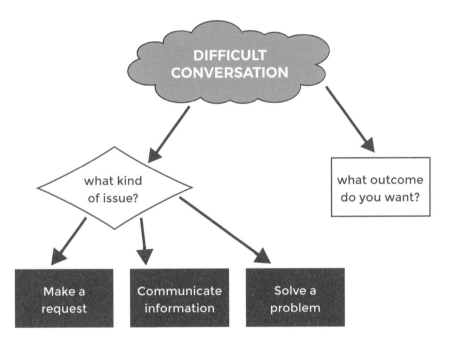

A single difficult conversation may have multiple issues.

Chris, a CEO, was having difficulties with his head of Sales, who had been in the role for six months and was not hitting his sales targets. Chris kept putting off the conversation he knew was necessary. On careful reflection, Chris's frustration with the Sales VP came down to these issues:

- The VP was not meeting his goals.

- It bothered Chris that the Sales VP was not taking initiative to correct the situation.

- Chris didn't want to have to tell the Sales VP what to do. As a senior executive, he was expected to solve the problem on his own.

What Chris wanted from the difficult conversation was to solve the problem (the VP missing sales targets) and to communicate the need for the VP to take the initiative.

Turn Problems into Outcome-Based Questions

When people encounter problems, the first question they often ask starts with "Why." A much more powerful way to address issues and get into action is to frame problems as outcome-based questions that start with "How" or "What."

Chris asked his Sales VP two questions: "What can you do to get back on track to hit your sales numbers next quarter?" and "How can you make up for this quarter's gap by the end of the year?"

If someone is struggling to keep up with his workload and falling behind, try "What can we do to rearrange your schedule or clear your calendar so you can get back on track with this high-priority item?"

2. CLARIFY YOUR DESIRED OUTCOME

Having sorted through the issues in the conversation ahead, identify the desired outcome for the conversation.

In our example, Chris faced two choices. Option A was to fire or demote the Sales executive. Option B was to manage the person in such a way that he would be effective—by making requests, managing results, offering advice, providing training, or increasing resources.

Chris realized that it was in the business's best interest to put aside the thought that "I shouldn't have to tell this person anything." The business would benefit if instead Chris offered support and worked with the executive to solve the problem.

Chris met with the Sales VP and together they mapped out a three-month plan with clear deliverables and milestones, and built regularly scheduled check-in and review meetings. By separating the needs of the business from his personal frustration, Chris was able to work with his VP to create an effective solution and clear path forward.

3. SHIFT PERSPECTIVES

The third part of preparing for a difficult conversation is to separate your own intentions, desires, and concerns from those of the other person in the conversation.

One way to do this is to act out the conversation using empty chairs. Set up three chairs in a room: two facing each other, and one to the side, as an observer. Think of a tennis court with two players facing each other and the chair umpire at the net, observing play.

Sit in the first chair, in your own role. Ask yourself questions about how you're approaching the conversation:

- "How do I see this situation? What is my objective?"

- "What do I see when I look across at the other person?"

Then switch to the other chair and sit for a moment as the person with whom you will have the difficult conversation. Try to put yourself in that person's position and mind-set. Then ask:

- "How do I see this situation as this person? What is my objective?"

- "What do I want as an outcome from this conversation?"

- "How do I see the person sitting across from me?"

The third chair represents an impartial observer or the embodiment of the business. Sit in this chair for a moment and think about what you have seen in the others. From this business perspective, ask yourself the following questions:

- "How do I see this situation as an outside, third-party observer?"

- "Having seen both sides objectively, what insights do I have into the situation?"

- "What advice would I give to both parties about how to proceed?"

Simply taking the time to think deeply from an outside perspective often reveals a great deal about the situation. Sitting in the other person's chair, you may understand her disappointment or anxiety. Perhaps you realize that the person has no idea of the problem and will feel blindsided. With insight into the other person's perspective, you can communicate with greater compassion.

By taking the third-party perspective, you put aside your own emotional involvement in the issues and may discover another resolution or a more constructive way to communicate unwelcome news.

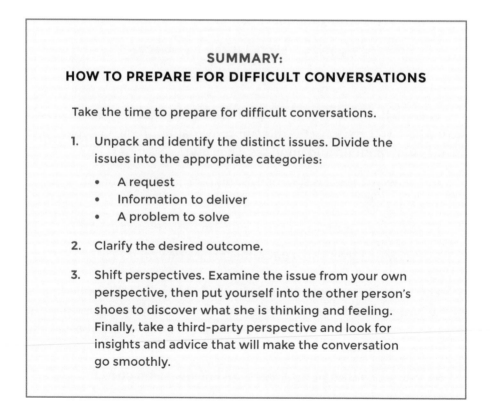

SUMMARY:
HOW TO PREPARE FOR DIFFICULT CONVERSATIONS

Take the time to prepare for difficult conversations.

1. Unpack and identify the distinct issues. Divide the issues into the appropriate categories:

   - A request
   - Information to deliver
   - A problem to solve

2. Clarify the desired outcome.

3. Shift perspectives. Examine the issue from your own perspective, then put yourself into the other person's shoes to discover what she is thinking and feeling. Finally, take a third-party perspective and look for insights and advice that will make the conversation go smoothly.

COMMUNICATE WITH COMPASSION AND CLARITY

For critical or extremely sensitive conversations, you might rehearse exactly how you will communicate.

If you have carefully separated the issues, clarify and distinguish them during the conversation. Where possible, separate the positive from the negative clearly so the other person will understand that you're looking at the entire picture, not just the difficult part.

One way to do this is to prepare comments with the following structure: "On the one hand . . . On the other hand . . ."

For example, if Chris is unhappy with the Sales VP's performance, he could put the problem into the larger context: "I know that you've only been in this role for a short while. On the one hand, you're doing a good job of motivating people in a difficult climate. On the other hand, you're not meeting the sales targets we agreed to, and have not given me a clear plan for reaching them."

CAUTION: Don't throw in positive comments that aren't genuine. Inauthentic praise will ring false, eroding trust. People are remarkably adept at seeing past words to what you really feel.

According to research by Albert Mehrabian, a former UCLA psychology professor, when nonverbal and verbal communications are not consistent, people pay attention largely to the nonverbal cues. In a face-to-face conversation, 55 percent of what we hear is determined by body language, 38 percent from tone of voice, and 7 percent from the actual words. If you don't really mean what you're saying, you're likely to give that away in your tone of voice or body language.

Separate the positive and negative to clarify the problem while you respect the other person's position and contributions.

MAKE ROOM FOR SILENCE

Silence can be an ally in difficult conversations. Strategically remaining quiet gives you time to regroup internally, to present an outward face of calm while you gather your thoughts and defuse an emotional reaction. Remaining silent at a difficult moment also prevents you from stepping on someone else's reaction, and offers the listener a chance to think and express a reaction.

We are wired to fill silences in conversations, particularly after delivering bad news or making a difficult request. We may want to short-circuit the listener's negative reaction, or defend ourselves. But remaining silent at this pivotal moment allows the other person to process the information. Anything other than silence can sound like an explanation, a story, or an excuse.

THE 10-SECOND RULE

Long, silent pauses are difficult to maintain because of our natural inclination to fill silence.

Try the 10-Second Rule in a difficult conversation. When the other person says something troubling or objects to your idea, don't utter a word for 10 seconds. Count in your head if necessary.

Watch what happens: often, the other person will jump in with another offer or reveal more information. Most people are uncomfortable with silence and will do anything to fill it. When you feel at home with 10 seconds of silence, you will naturally use silence frequently as a strategic tool. You'll be amazed by the results.

Facebook and Google were quietly recruiting one of our clients, the head of an industry business unit at a tech company. He had not received a significant raise in his current job in more than five years, and the opportunities being presented to him were at a substantially higher salary.

He loved working at his current company and didn't want to leave. He met with his boss to make a request for a salary increase. He named the specific salary target he wanted, and made three points to substantiate his request. Then he said, "I don't want to respond to calls from Facebook and Google," and shut up. He reported that waiting in silence was excruciating. Finally his boss said, "I knew this was an issue. Thank you for making me pay attention to it. You're one of our most critical employees, and I will make this happen."

CHAPTER 23

FROM BREAKDOWN TO BREAKTHROUGH

How to Resolve Problems

"Houston, we have a problem."

Get ready to hear the business equivalent of that famous update from the Apollo 13 mission. Moonshots reveal problems and breakdowns.

Problems and breakdowns create an opportunity to strengthen team performance and open the door to revolutionary ideas and heroic contributions. But if not handled effectively, they can tear teams apart, polarize staff, and create a culture of fear and risk aversion.

> **66** NASA presented the astronauts as robots. In fact they are not robots. They are men who have an extraordinary balance between disciplines and daredevilry. Robots could not have gone to the moon because a robot breaks down the moment there is a fluctuation in the current. **99**
>
> NORMAN MAILER,
> *Moonfire, The Epic Journey of Apollo 11*

ADDRESS THE RIGHT PROBLEMS

The everyday work environment presents a host of potential difficulties, including personnel problems, communication failures, team dysfunction, customer complaints, and technical glitches. In a business-as-usual setting, we spend all of our time buried in issues that present themselves as problems.

Effective teams and leaders are adept at identifying and focusing on the problems that interfere with their ability to achieve critical business results rather than addressing minor issues. Most problems occupy one of three severity levels:

- **An issue** is something that's not optimal and that may get in the way of progress. For example: *The engineering and marketing teams are not working well together.*

- **A business problem** is a barrier between the current situation and the stated objective. For example: *We're not on track to deliver our beta release on July 31.*

- **A breakdown** is a business problem that you cannot see a way to solve. For example: *The product failed to pass our drop tests and needs to be redesigned.*

Smaller issues sometimes point to larger problems. To make sure you're not missing a critical problem, ask clarifying questions to discover whether an issue threatens the broader goal. For example:

- "What specifically do you mean when you say that the engineering and marketing teams are not working well together?"

- "What impact does this have on the overall project?"

- "How will we know when engineering and marketing are working well together?"

- "What results will you see in the business when that happens?"

Most issues and problems can be resolved when they are defined and given appropriate attention. Breakdowns, on the other hand, are major business problems with no obvious solutions. If not resolved, breakdowns derail moonshots. Unlike business-as-usual issues, breakdowns warrant thoughtful consideration, including whether to change the goal, or even abandon the project.

THREE RESPONSES TO A BREAKDOWN

A breakdown offers three possible courses of action.

1. **CHANGE THE GOAL.** Change or redefine the objective or move the deadline. When changing a milestone, assess how the change might affect other milestones and the ultimate goal.

2. **ABANDON THE GOAL.** Sometimes the right thing to do is to stop working on a goal, particularly when external events alter the business or competitive landscape or when information becomes available that disrupts underlying assumptions or overarching objectives.

3. **FIND A BREAKTHROUGH.** Get the team together to tackle the crisis and find a way through.

The appropriate action depends on the situation, the team ethics and mission rules, and broader business interests. Delaying a ship date or changing an interim objective might be required to sustain momentum over the long haul.

NASA rescheduled many launch dates due to bad weather and equipment malfunction.

The lunar module had the most technical issues of all the components of the Apollo system. In June 1968, it was behind schedule when it was shipped to the Kennedy Space Center, and the team discovered more than 100 defects. Grumman Aircraft Engineering Corporation, the lead contractor for the lunar module, had estimated that it would not be ready until at least February 1969, which would delay the entire program.

George Low, manager of the Apollo Spacecraft Program Office, proposed a solution in August 1968. Since the command service module (CSM) would be ready three months before the lunar module, instead of flying the CSM on an early mission in Earth orbit, Low proposed they skip the Earth orbit mission and send the CSM all the way to the moon. This new mission would allow NASA to practice procedures for lunar flight that would otherwise have to wait for a later mission. The Central Intelligence Agency had concerns that the Soviet Union was planning its own circumlunar flight for December to upstage the Americans. The Earth orbit mission was cancelled, and astronaut Frank Borman's crew was chosen to fly the CSM lunar orbit mission on Apollo 8.

(The swap of crews was decisive in determining who would be the first person to walk on the moon. Pete Conrad was backup commander for James McDivitt's crew, and by the process of crew rotation would have been in line to be the commander of Apollo 11. Neil Armstrong instead received this honor because he was Borman's backup commander.)

When a breakdown happens, consider whether abandoning the plan altogether is the right approach. For example, market or marketplace conditions may have changed and as a result, your product or solution may no longer be competitive. Or, knowing what you know now, the fastest and most efficient way forward may be to decide to start over and take an entirely different approach.

Abandoning a project, while not the optimal choice, is often over-looked as a viable option. Killing projects that aren't working frees resources and focus for other initiatives or a different moonshot. Smart leaders become as adept at making decisions about what *not* to do as they are about making decisions about what to do.

If you choose to change or abandon the goal, make sure everyone on the team understands that you've reached this decision as a result of a conscious and measured consideration. Too often, we let milestones slip, then abandon projects without sufficient communication or closure. To get the most out of the effort invested to date, discuss the rationale behind the change in plans, share lessons learned, and acknowledge the efforts that have brought you this far.

In some situations, you have no choice but to find another way through a daunting problem, or a workaround. To find workarounds and breakthroughs, teams need to put blame aside and collaborate on a common goal.

THE PATH TO A BREAKTHROUGH

A breakdown might feel like a crisis, but it may also present a golden opportunity.

In the history of Apollo missions, few breakdowns were more sustained and dramatic than the aftermath of the oxygen tank explosion during the Apollo 13 mission, while the crew was en route to the moon. Mission Control instantly abandoned the initial mission plan and adopted another: bringing the crew safely home. Achieving that mission required multiple breakthroughs.

"Houston, we have a problem." This was the astronaut's statement after an explosion during the Apollo 13 mission damaged oxygen tanks in the spacecraft. Since oxygen fed the spacecraft's power source, power was reduced and the spacecraft became inoperable. Luckily the damaged *Odyssey* spacecraft had a backup: the *Aquarius* lunar module. The astronauts switched to *Aquarius* for the trip home.

However, *Aquarius* had problems with the CO_2 "scrubbers," the lithium hydroxide canisters that filtered carbon dioxide from the cabin of the lunar module. Jerry Woodfill, who helped design and monitor the Apollo 13 caution and warning systems, was summoned to join a tiger team led by Ed Smylie, the crew's systems manager, to solve the problem. "There were but two round lithium hydroxide canisters in the LM, able to provide filtering for two men for two days," said Woodfill. "With the trip back to Earth at least four days in length, and three men on board, the carbon dioxide content of the cabin air would rise to poisonous levels, and the crew would expire without a solution."

They had 24 hours to solve the problem.

Using only the type of equipment and tools the crew had on board, Smylie and his team came up with a solution. "The concept . . . was to attach a suit hose into a port which blew air through the hose into an astronaut's space suit," said Woodfill. "If the space suit was eliminated and, instead, the output of the hose somehow attached to the square filter, perhaps, the crew could be saved. The air blown through the filter by the suit fan would have no carbon dioxide as it reentered the cabin atmosphere."

The biggest challenge was how to attach the hose with a small round inlet hole into a much larger square outlet attached and surrounding the square air filter. Their solution was to "use cardboard log book covers to support the plastic," said Woodfill. "It worked!" To attach the funnel to prevent leaking, they used a supply that had been stowed on board every mission since the early 1960s, duct tape.

After the solution was tested and proven in the simulators at Mission Control, the team radioed instructions to the crew and led them through about an hour's worth of steps. As Jim Lovell wrote in his book *Lost Moon*, the duct tape solution that saved Apollo 13 "wasn't very handsome, but it worked."

In the words of Gene Kranz, flight director for both Apollo 11 and Apollo 13:

These three astronauts were beyond our physical reach. But not beyond the reach of human imagination, inventiveness, and a creed that we all lived by: "Failure is not an option."

Breakdowns often happen suddenly, due to events outside of our control. They appear as unexpected failures, PR disasters, unanticipated moves by a competitor (such as moonshots of their own), or insurmountable technology barriers.

We cannot prevent problems but we can control how we handle them.

Since the dawn of human history, people have reacted to surprises and potential threats with a "fight-or-flight" response. Because teams and organizations are made up of humans, they follow the same pattern when faced with a serious breakdown.

When stuck in business-as-usual mode, most people's reaction to a crisis follows three stages:

1. **PANIC:** The "Oh s***!" moment. People rush around, spread the news in hushed tones, and let the full crisis sink in as everyone experiences the fight-or-flight response.

2. **BLAME:** Once the initial shock wears off, people naturally spend time and energy looking for the source of the problem and who is to blame. Blame grows out of defensiveness. When we're worried about being right, we have to find someone who is wrong.

3. **RESOLUTION:** After traveling through the orbits of panic and blame, most teams then eventually get around to fixing the problem, usually in "damage-control" mode.

But there's a better way to handle a breakdown—one that pulls teams together rather than tearing them apart. High-performing teams and forward-thinking leaders stay relentlessly focused on the future outcome, and that changes everything.

The three phases of handling a breakdown effectively and proactively are as follows:

1. **ASSESS THE CURRENT SITUATION:** What's the current situation? What has happened or is happening right now? What is the impact?

2. **EXPLORE POSSIBILITIES:** Given the current situation, what options are available to us? What outcomes are possible? Use this opportunity to explore possibilities that may not have been considered before.

3. **COMMIT TO A COURSE OF ACTION:** Having brainstormed possibilities, what action will the team now take to resolve the problem and achieve a desired outcome?

This approach focuses energy and creativity on finding opportunities, not assessing blame. Bypassing blame reduces defensiveness and opens the path to collaboration and innovation. Rather than damage control, this process typically results in greater possibility and opportunity.

Teams can change their approach to a breakdown from reactive to proactive in mid-course by shifting the focus from blame and explanation to possibilities and outcomes. When those around you ask about *why* the problem happened, focus the conversation instead on what you now know and how you intend to move forward. Put aside the question of blame and redirect the conversation to consider a range of possible actions. For example:

> "We'll address that question in the post-mortem, after we've taken action. For now, let's focus on the solution and outcomes ahead, not the actions behind us."

Watch Your Questions

Throughout the process of addressing a crisis, choose questions carefully to remain forward-focused and proactive. Be aware, however, that the pull of the reactive approach is very strong.

- Put aside the *who* or *why* questions, as they maintain a focus on the past.

- Ask only *what* or *how* questions to keep the focus on the present and the future.

There is a time and place to look for causes and learn from mistakes. NASA debriefed crews on phases of the mission even as the mission progressed, and again after splashdown. Technical teams hold post-mortems for launches. But the time for the post-mortem is *after* the crisis, not during it.

In January 1967, a fire broke out during a pre-flight test for the first crewed flight of Apollo, which was scheduled to launch in February. The three astronauts aboard, Virgil Grissom, Edward White, and Roger Chaffee, lost their lives.

Immediately after the fire, to avoid the appearance of a conflict of interest, James E. Webb asked President Lyndon B. Johnson to allow NASA to handle the investigation, and promised to keep the appropriate leaders of Congress informed. NASA convened the Apollo 204 Accident Review Board, and both houses of Congress initiated their own committee inquiries to oversee the NASA review.

The cause was determined to be an electrical fire that ignited combustible nylon material in the high-pressure, oxygen-rich cabin atmosphere. The astronauts could not be rescued because the door hatch would not open against internal pressure.

The review also concluded that because the test was unfueled, NASA did not identify the test as hazardous, and thus the tragedy was hampered by poor emergency preparedness. The board concluded that the emergency equipment (such as gas masks) were inadequate; that fire, rescue, and medical teams were not in attendance; and that the spacecraft access areas contained many obstacles to emergency response such as steps, sliding doors, and sharp turns.

Manned flights were suspended for 20 months while the hazards were corrected based on the recommendations of the review committee. Because the committee focused on solutions and not blame, they discovered all of the opportunities to improve the process. Just nine months after the accident, the first successful manned Apollo mission, flown by the backup crew, launched in October 1968.

CREATE OR ANTICIPATE A BREAKDOWN

A crisis creates an opportunity to galvanize teams and transform how people operate together. When you realize the power of a breakdown to generate breakthroughs, you might be tempted to cause one intentionally. Great leaders often do.

> 66 Until I said the target was zero, we didn't have a problem. Part of the role of leadership is to create a crisis. 99
>
> PAUL O'NEILL,
> ALCOA

A breakdown forces teams out of their usual patterns and spurs creative thinking about outcomes. Breakdowns deliver positive results when you take the proactive, outcome-based approach to handling the crisis.

Using this strategy, you can choose to manufacture a breakdown to open doors to innovation, creative thinking, and risk-taking.

WARNING: Forcing breakdowns using shame and blame will backfire, disrupt team performance, and create a risk-averse culture.

When you look carefully at the three phases, you may discover that you can generate a breakthrough without ever experiencing a crisis. These steps work equally well for more typical business problems:

1. Assess the situation—with or without a breakdown.

2. Brainstorm what's possible for the situation.

3. Choose a course of action that meets a desired outcome.

Some great leaders anticipate a breakdown to avoid it altogether, or substitute a success for a failure. For example:

- "We just took the market-leading position. Now everyone's gunning for us—what should we do?"

- "We've just signed our biggest customer ever. How can we make sure that they're completely happy with their customer experience?"

GE's "Ecomagination" moonshot spurred immediate, company-wide breakthroughs because it required the company to cut resource usage in its existing plants and facilities. The "Ecomagination" team conducted "treasure hunts" to find ways to increase efficiencies using their own products. The team replaced a factory's old sodium halide lights with compact fluorescent bulbs. A team in Ohio saved 3 million gallons of fuel a year by moving aircraft engine testing inside. The company then shared its breakthroughs with customers so they, too, could cut down on energy use.

When you proactively look for new possibilities from your current situation, you can create a breakthrough without waiting for a crisis.

CREATING A BREAKDOWN
WITH A TINY PIECE OF PAPER

Mr. K had no background in the hospitality business when he was appointed head of an international luxury hotel conglomerate. He had previously been a successful executive in financial services, and brought his leadership and management acumen to bear in this new role. He knew that the hotel had lost its competitive edge and reputation for excellence, but he relied on the creativity of his staff to reverse the decline. And he created breakdowns internally, before they happened in front of hotel guests.

Partway through the morning of an all-day staff meeting, he stopped the meeting to point out a small piece of paper on the floor, which everyone had walked past without noticing. *How could this happen in a hotel with the highest standards for service and excellence?* He threw the agenda aside and took the entire executive team on a tour of the hotel's supply closets, where housekeeping staff accessed linens and supplies. The closets were in disarray. He noted every infraction in each supply and linen closet on all 26 floors. He turned these minor, hidden issues into a high-priority crisis.

Mr. K manufactured a breakdown by identifying small problems that were inconsistent with his vision of running the finest hotel in the city. In doing so, he recalibrated expectations for excellence, and set the bar higher.

The approach worked. His staff internalized these higher standards, creating new processes to elevate operations. The hotel has since regained its reputation for excellence, boasting the number-one ranking in its city of 13 million people.

THREE SECRETS TO GENERATING BREAKTHROUGHS

Once you understand the difference between proactive and reactive approaches to crisis, you can take advantage of the power of breakdowns to create breakthroughs.

1. Switch from reactive to proactive responses at any moment by changing from backward-facing *who* and *why* questions to forward-looking *how* and *what* questions.

2. Manufacture a breakdown from the inside to stimulate a breakthrough.

3. Once teams know how to work together to create breakthroughs, don't wait for a crisis; start looking for positive ways to disrupt business as usual.

PART FOUR

Entrepreneurs

S tarting a business is a bold endeavor. The odds are stacked against success. Startup failure rate statistics vary, but generally, it's 75 to 90 percent. It takes courage to follow an uncharted course with limited fuel and a tight time frame.

As with most moonshots, the path ahead is not easy—if it were, many would have traveled it ahead of you. To improve your chances of success, set out with the right tools and practices.

Coming up with a product or service idea may be the easiest part of the startup. As an entrepreneur, you'll make critical decisions in assembling a startup team and creating an environment for successful execution. Your tasks include finding the right advisors and keeping everyone working toward the shared vision. Business growth demands resilience and creativity to find breakthroughs and change course when needed.

The chapters in this section outline practices that set entrepreneurs and startups on a path to a successful moonshot. While these practices apply in any business setting, we've found them to be particularly important when pursuing a moonshot.

- **CULTIVATE BREAKTHROUGHS:** Systems for solving intractable problems

- **FROM ENTREPRENEUR TO LEADER:** Become the leader the business needs

- **THE LAUNCH TEAM:** Assemble the crew

- **MISSION RULES FOR STARTUPS:** Build the company you want to run

- **STARTUP STORIES:** The entrepreneur as storyteller

- **IN-FLIGHT OPERATIONS:** Stay on course

- **CALL IN THE ROCKET SCIENTISTS:** Ask for advice

- **REPORT TO GROUND CONTROL:** Manage your boards and investors

CULTIVATE BREAKTHROUGHS

Systems for Solving Intractable Problems

To get to the moon, NASA and its contractors had to solve multitudes of mind-bending problems. They accomplished what seemed impossible time and again, working through major setbacks, including misfires and explosions.

A startup likewise faces insurmountable odds. Consider how many businesses fail. If you looked at the odds alone, you might head to a craps table instead. Entrepreneurs know that they will endure difficult breakdowns and problems. Yet they stay the course and look past the failures to a vision of what's possible.

Creating breakthroughs is the core business of a startup.

The most successful startups are those that take the inevitable breakdowns in stride and put systems in place to resolve them.

Barry Eggers, the founding partner of Lightspeed Venture Partners, cites problem solving as a critical success factor for startups. "When evaluating investing in startups, one of the key things we try to get a sense for is how they approach and solve problems, especially those that pose significant obstacles to their business," says Eggers. "A defined, repeatable process for effective problem solving in a founding team is a strong indicator of future success."

We define a breakdown as a problem that threatens the company's ability to achieve one or more core business objectives, and is so significant that you cannot see a way around it. There are three possible responses to this kind of breakdown:

1. Change the objective

2. Abandon the objective

3. Find a breakthrough

Startups tend to be consumed by difficult technical challenges, and thus find it necessary to manufacture breakthroughs more frequently than established businesses. How do leaders create an environment in which breakthroughs can happen? Create systems and processes.

This chapter discusses essential strategies for turning your startup into a problem-solving, innovating, breakthrough machine that shoots for the moon:

- Replicate successes in other domains

- Find lead users

- Ask powerful questions

- Launch experiments

REPLICATE SUCCESSES IN OTHER DOMAINS

The answer to your problem may lie outside your area of expertise. Look for other industries or situations that share similar characteristics and see what works for them. Repurpose other practices for your own reasons.

A small company needed to hire 30 people for a three-month stretch to produce a global online event. The act of hiring 30 people using business-as-usual processes would take months that the company did not have.

Instead, the company decided to treat the opportunity like a casting call for a Broadway show. The hiring team published a list of job descriptions and announced the hiring day. It leased an auditorium in downtown San Francisco for the event. On the interview day, the line of people extended down the street. Prospective hires listened to a presentation about the company and project. The hiring team sorted candidates for the different roles, sent them through interviews, and scored them. At the end of the day, the team met and, like directors casting a show, made their decisions. Within the week, all 30 positions were filled.

If you're calling in outside experts, consider looking beyond your own industry, based on the underlying attributes of the market. And remember that inspiration—and solutions—can be found in unlikely places.

For example, neonatal incubators provide essential care for premature babies, yet in developing countries, they are rarely used because no one has the knowledge or parts to repair them when they break. Recognizing this fact, the nonprofit Design that Matters turned to auto mechanics to create the NeoNurture incubator. The resulting incubator is crafted from parts such as headlights, dashboard fans, motorcycle batteries, and door chimes. By looking outside the medical domain, the company created a product that fits easily into the local economy, which was well stocked with both repair expertise and spare parts.

FIND LEAD USERS

Another way to fuel breakthroughs is to tap into the creativity and in-the-field expertise of people at the leading edge of your industry. Look within your domain but outside your company at the most innovative of your potential customers.

3M as a company has a history of sustained innovation and repeated breakthroughs. The company has embraced a Lead User Methodology for manufacturing advances. Based on research that shows that many commercially successful products are initially patched together by users and potential customers, 3M collaborates with innovative individuals from outside the business as "lead users" on cross-functional teams tasked with creating breakthroughs.

The company tested the lead-user process while developing a surgical drape product for the Medical-Surgical Markets division. Surgical drapes are films that adhere to a patient's skin during surgery, providing important protection against contamination and infection. As an adhesive product, they are clearly in 3M's sweet spot and undisputed expertise. The company searched for a breakthrough to make the technology more affordable for developing markets, where infectious diseases are rampant.

3M's cross-functional team traveled the world, working with surgeons and other medical professionals in developing countries, veterinarians, and Hollywood makeup artists. These people all shared a common interest in maintaining sterile conditions in vastly different environments and applications. They identified a group of lead users, with whom they brainstormed on innovations in surgical draping. The result was a series of ideas for advancing the medical draping business.

To use the lead-user process, you'll need to commit to working with users and clearly define the legal ownership of ideas generated. (3M made it clear to participants that the company owned the intellectual property that resulted from the project.) Build cross-functional teams to drive the breakthrough, and have them reach out through their networks to find people in the field. Have team members ask their own networks for references, and use expanding circles of connection to find people in the potential user or customer community that are innovative and willing to work together to create new products or services.

ASK POWERFUL QUESTIONS

The first response to a breakdown or a seemingly insurmountable problem is to adopt the stance that you *can* and *will* solve the problem. The belief that you will find a solution inspires the creative thought that fuels breakthroughs. Call your team together and ask "How" or "What" questions that focus on the future, rather than the past. Create a list of at least 10 questions for which the answers would contribute to a solution. In other words, if you could have answers to any 10 questions, what questions would you ask?

For example, a sales team that has not met revenue goals might ask:

1. How can we generate a robust sales pipeline?

2. How can we reduce the cost of acquiring new customers?

3. How can we more quickly qualify customers so we don't waste time selling to customers who won't buy?

4. How can we reduce the time and resources required to produce custom bids for each prospect?

5. How can we increase our conversion rate from prospect to customer?

6. What might we do to cut the sales cycle in half?

7. How could we shift the focus of our internal resources to enable us to meet our revenue goals?

8. What are the attributes of our ideal customer?

9. How can we price our product to achieve greater market penetration?

10. What product packaging options might lead to greater market penetration?

LAUNCH A SERIES OF EXPERIMENTS

Having an experimental mind-set is one way to build resilience into your business. Experimentation is also the path to breakthrough. When you formalize experimentation as part of the business culture, you have these processes already in place when you need to create a breakthrough.

When seeking a breakthrough, consider launching a scientific experiment and making data-driven decisions. By calling the effort an experiment, you're framing the outcome, whether positive or negative, as an expected part of a learning process. Even if your first attempt fails, you learn something that may move you closer to a solution. When failure is acceptable and even welcome, people have the freedom to think more creatively and propose divergent ideas—the stuff from which breakthroughs are made.

Startup Fictiv has formalized its process of experimentation. Says CEO Dave Evans, "For every test we run, we have an experiment report with a hypothesis. If an experiment proves the hypothesis to be false, it's still a success." Fictiv posts the results of its experiments for everyone in the company to see, and presents awards for experiments that yield significant insights and contribute to solving critical problems.

When crafting an experiment, model the scientific method as much as possible in the following manner:

1. Ask a question directly related to the problem you want to solve. For example:

    *   What experiments will we run to determine whether our product has the right minimum viable product feature set for our target customers?

    *   What experiments will we run to increase the conversion from prospect to customer?

2. Do some research; this is where you might reach outside your domain for inspiration.

3. Construct a hypothesis that you want to prove or disprove.

4. Test the hypothesis. Real-world experimentation is rarely as clean as laboratory conditions, but you can find ways to test within your own domain, using A/B testing, a method of comparing two options against each other to determine which one performs better, or employ other strategies to isolate the performance of specific factors.

5. Analyze your data and draw a conclusion. Have you proven or disproved your hypothesis? Look deeper, if possible; the data may reveal results outside of the hypothesis, providing the groundwork for the next experiment.

6. Communicate your results. Experiments are worthless if you do not learn from them. Sharing the results amplifies their value to your business.

FROM ENTREPRENEUR TO LEADER

Become the Leader the Business Needs

Entrepreneurship has many faces; there are no hard-and-fast rules about who can start a business. Age, gender, and cultural limitations do not apply. In recent years, crowdfunding capabilities have lowered financial barriers as well.

Between business inception and sustained success, many entrepreneurs take on leadership responsibilities. Founders become CEOs or COOs, often for the first time in their careers, and develop alongside the businesses they build.

A startup's growth trajectory depends on how people inhabit leadership roles, making the transition from founders and colleagues to startup executives and visionary leaders. Often, startup leaders earn their place in the business due to domain expertise, not leadership experience.

Nothing develops leaders like a moonshot.

Decision-making is often a challenge for founding teams that are relatively new to leadership. Inexperienced leaders struggle to know when to take charge and when to let others take the lead. This chapter offers guidance for founders about how to develop leadership skills as they build businesses.

HOW DO YOU MAKE DECISIONS?

A prominent Silicon Valley venture capitalist who listens to many startup pitches told us that he asks each startup team a simple question: "How do you make decisions?"

Some teams cannot answer the question. Others declare, "We decide everything by consensus." In either case, this VC sees warning signs of a startup team that might not execute well under the pressure as business dynamics change and they grapple with rapid growth.

Consensus may sound ideal, but in the harsh reality of a startup, it can lead to delays and poor decisions. When everyone has input and every vote counts equally, decision-making takes too long. The company may fall behind or miss critical, fleeting opportunities. Worse, consensus often leads to mediocrity because it favors the decision everyone can agree on, which may not be the best course of action.

Agility is a startup's key advantage over established businesses. Ruling by consensus erodes this advantage, paralyzing decision-making. To pivot and react quickly, startups must be able to make decisions rapidly. The key is for a leader to remain humble and act with respect when making tough calls.

Gathering opinions and collaboration are vital. But decision authority ultimately rests with *someone*. As you define the roles and responsibilities of the founding team, clearly delineate who owns each of the critical decisions, such as budget approval and establishing development priorities.

This shift can be difficult for the entrepreneur stepping into the CEO role for the first time. As founder of Judicata, Itai Gurari describes his experience as follows: "When we started, we wanted to be collaborative. My background in law and philosophy made me believe in the power of persuasion. I've come to realize that persuasion is not always possible; there are times I need to make the hard call and make a decision, whether or not everyone agrees."

THE ACCIDENTAL EXECUTIVE

Many entrepreneurs and startup founders suffer from the Accidental Executive Mind-Set—the belief that they aren't qualified to run a company. And truthfully, many lack the skills and experience to lead effectively.

Don't let that stop you.

John F. Kennedy was only months into his presidency, untested at one of the most challenging leadership jobs imaginable, when he staked out the mission to the moon. Doing so defined his leadership style and his legacy. Managing a moonshot can do the same for you.

Companies that disrupt industries aren't led by the usual people doing the usual things. It's okay to break the mold when reinventing business as usual.

With the right advisors and mentors, you will learn on the job. A startup is an ideal vehicle for developing leadership capacity.

If you're new to leadership in your startup, adopt the following practices:

- Hone your resilience

- Lead like a hippo

- Be confidently humble

BE A RESILIENT LEARNER

The most important thing a startup founder can bring to the table isn't technical brilliance, a great idea, or sales prowess. It's resilience. Every startup endures setbacks and breakdowns. The successful ones survive and learn from them.

The resilient entrepreneur regulates negative feedback and turns problems into learning opportunities. Setbacks ultimately develop strength, while mistakes and failure lead to growth.

Resilience comes from within, with emotional resources and maturity. It develops with experience, which is why a startup failure can enhance an entrepreneur's value. You can actively cultivate resilience by adopting the right attitudes and practices from the start.

Become a student of leadership. The most successful first-time leaders are those who approach the experience as a learning opportunity.

In her research into responses to failure, Professor Carol Dweck of Stanford University identifies a *growth mind-set* as a critical factor to resilience and success. People with a growth mind-set believe that they can change and grow through experience and practice. They see failures or struggles as an opportunity to learn. In the business world, the growth mind-set translates into powerful leadership.

The leader with a growth mind-set is open to coaching and feedback. He or she is not afraid of making mistakes, and asks for guidance.

"One of the key things I look for in a founder is their competence as a learner. Startup companies change at hyperbolic speed," says Sarah Tavel, partner at Greylock Partners. "Founders and executives who don't possess a learning mindset get left behind by the company. Being a learner means you have the humility to be wrong. You can't learn unless you admit that you don't know something."

Build resilience into the culture. Entrepreneurs can build resilience into the business structure itself, making it safe for others to take risks. The Lean Startup methodology defined by Eric Ries, a Silicon Valley entrepreneur and author, entails iteratively testing assumptions and quickly learning from failures by making necessary adjustments. Treat the startup experience as a series of experiments. Some experiments will fail and others will succeed; that is the nature of experimentation. In an experimental context, every failure advances knowledge.

"A lot of successful startup companies seem like overnight successes. But behind every one is a founding team that has been working day in and day out, often for years," said Tavel. "What seems so easy from the outside requires an incredible amount of persistence and resilience. I call that grit, and that's what I look for in the teams I fund."

LEAD LIKE A HIPPO

With the launch team in place, a startup entrepreneur does well to emulate the hippopotamus; stay mostly underwater, with eyes peering above the surface, observing. Don't draw attention to your presence. Emerge when needed to make a decision.

An adaptive leader steps in when needed to break deadlocks or move things forward, trusting others to contribute and lead.

The hippopotamus metaphor comes from a CEO who wants his employees to feel comfortable taking risks and trying things. He maintains his "underwater hippo" posture while his teams brainstorm and voice their opinions. He doesn't step up and take charge until there is a problem or until it is time to guide the discussion or make a decision.

If you have the right people in the right roles, and all are accountable for their areas of responsibility, then your role as a leader is to be present, observant, and supportive.

Adaptive leadership fills the power void,
but leaves space for creativity and innovation.

Effective brainstorming requires that people feel empowered to speak up and contribute to the discussion. This is the time to step back as a leader. When the team needs to tap your expertise or a make decision, step in to keep things moving.

Adaptive leadership flourishes when you have the right team in place and can trust the team to execute. This stance can be challenging for a first-time leader, but it pays dividends. A strong leader is adept at both stepping forward to lead and stepping back to share leadership.

BE CONFIDENTLY HUMBLE

Startups founded by groups of friends or colleagues often cherish egalitarian ideals. But as the business grows, someone has to step up to the role of CEO.

When you become that ultimate decision-maker, you're no longer one of the gang. Your words and behavior affect those around you and the very fabric of the business itself.

Don't underestimate the impact of your leadership style on your team and the business. Whether you realize it or not, when you're at the top, you're always leading by example.

This advice isn't meant to make you feel powerful. If anything, it's meant to remind you of the magnitude of your responsibility. The best leaders for creative, innovative, and risk-taking environments practice *confident humility*.

Confidence: Employees want visionary leaders who project confidence, make decisions, and promote the vision and the business. People will hesitate to take risks or innovate when they're not confident in their leader.

Humility: Leaders in startup environments need to empower people to be creative to contribute to their fullest. The best leaders submerge their egos and listen to those around them, remaining open to advice and input, and sharing credit and success with others.

> 66 **Truly perfect is becoming comfortable with your imperfections on the way to doing something remarkable.** 99
>
> SETH GODIN,
> author and marketing expert

THE STUDENT OF LEADERSHIP:
AARON LEVIE AT BOX

With his youthful face, unruly hair, and red sneakers, Aaron Levie is an unlikely CEO figure for an enterprise IT company. Business-as-usual wisdom dictates that enterprise IT buyers want staid, mature leaders for their key technology vendors. Many investors would have advised the founders to install a senior executive—someone with a track record and, ideally, a few gray hairs.

Yet more than half of the Fortune 500 businesses use Box, the company that Levie started from his college dorm at age 19 with co-founder Dylan Smith, another college student. Today, Box has successfully navigated the transition to the public markets.

Levie's career grew along with the company; in 2013, *Inc.* magazine named him Entrepreneur of the Year. His career is a lesson in the practices outlined in this chapter.

RESILIENT LEARNING: Perhaps because he started the business as a college student, Levie approached the experience of becoming a CEO with a learner's mind-set. To compensate for his lack of business experience, he actively built a network of advisors, including luminaries such as Cisco CEO John Chambers and Jeff Immelt of GE. He reads extensively and remains open to learning from coaches, mentors, and advisors.

According to Karen Appleton, one of the founding team at Box, "Aaron brought his vision to life for others, and worked on his presentation over and over again. He adjusted it after every meeting he was in."

CONFIDENT HUMILITY: Instead of approaching the CEO role with uncertainty or arrogance, Levie inhabits it with his own personality. An irrepressible sense of humor surfaces even as he speaks passionately about trends in enterprise IT. He'll wear a business suit at a public event, pairing it with red sneakers. Says Appleton, "He has mastered the art of being smart, humble, and energized at the same time." This attitude permeates Box corporate culture, communicating that enterprise software doesn't have to be boring.

PROTECT YOUR TIME

In the early days of a startup, everyone occupies multiple roles. Startup founders often stretch far beyond their initial expertise. As the business grows, effective CEOs learn to protect their time and energy.

An overstressed CEO is a startup liability.

Eager to keep things going, startup CEOs roll up their sleeves and dive into the work. They may spend time compensating for underperforming team members. Or perhaps they don't trust others around them enough to delegate tasks. Either way, important, long-term decisions and actions get sidetracked when the CEO is consumed by urgent, tactical activities.

If you're too busy to think strategically about the business and its course, ask yourself these questions:

1. Do I have the right people in place to manage and scale the critical parts of the business?

2. What am I spending my time on now that I could delegate if the right person were available?

3. What are the things that only I am equipped to do? Am I spending enough time on these activities? Am I leveraging my strengths?

Identify the areas and tasks that are consuming your time and can be handled by others with little training or oversight, and create a plan to offload them. If you don't have the right people to take them on, start hiring. The most effective leaders are adept at identifying tasks suited for others. If internal resources aren't available, they work with consultants to clear the decks.

If you're worried about the expense of bringing on more people, evaluate the cost of *not* taking action. Ask yourself a fourth question about the current situation:

4. What would I contribute to the business if I could spend my time and energy on the things that only I can do?

As the CEO of a growing business, you are a crucial resource in the business. Your time is limited and precious. Preserve your time and energy for the tasks that require your attention and abilities, such as long-term planning, hiring, and strategic decisions, partnerships, and negotiations.

With the right people in place, a startup can operate more effectively and scale up more quickly. Recruit the right launch team and hire early and strategically.

CHAPTER 26

THE LAUNCH TEAM

Assemble the Crew

The Apollo missions each had three-person crews: two pilots and one commander. The carefully selected team trained closely together. Everyone clearly understood their responsibilities, and trusted and depended on each other.

A startup demands the same clarity and trust among its founding team.

In his book *The Founder's Dilemma*, Noam Wasserman suggests that more than half of startups fail due to problems with people, such as leadership issues, relationship conflicts, lack of clarity about roles, and poor decision-making. Even when startups attribute failures to other issues, such as running out of money or not listening to the market requirements, many of those problems trace their origins to dysfunctional team dynamics.

The people you bring with you will determine the success of the mission. The first task of the startup is getting the crew on board. This includes:

- Choosing the right people to build a productive team

- Creating an organizational structure that promotes innovation and resilience

- Defining roles and responsibilities for effective operations

RECRUIT A DIVERSE CREW

In her research into startup success, leadership, and teams, Professor Lindy Greer of the Stanford Graduate School of Business finds that most startups make a vital mistake in their early days: assembling a startup team that lacks diversity of skills and personal attributes. A possible explanation for this? We tend to gravitate toward people with whom we have a lot in common.

High-performing startups thrive when their team members have complementary and diverse skill sets.

When the core team shares the overlapping skills, people tend to compare their contributions and efforts, planting seeds of conflict later on. For example, if every member of a founding startup team is a software engineer, people may compare the relative worth of their contributions. (Watch a few episodes of HBO's *Silicon Valley* to see what this looks like.) Worse, the business will lack financial, business development, marketing, and other skills sets it needs.

Cross-functional teams bring unique experience and contribute within different areas of responsibilities. Individuals feel empowered to take responsibility for their area of expertise, and respect and depend on each other's contributions.

As CEO and co-founder of startup Fictiv, Dave Evans believes team diversity contributes to innovation. "When people from the same backgrounds work together, they develop narrow solutions. When people share a common thread with diverse experience and backgrounds, they develop products that reflect that diversity."

Even on cross-functional teams, the launch team members must work together well. Often, alignment is forged through common values and a shared vision for the startup. Says Greer, "Strive for diversity in expertise and similarity in values. On a diverse team, visionary leadership aligns everyone."

DEFINE THE ORGANIZATIONAL STRUCTURE

One of the first tasks of the startup team is defining the organizational structure for the business as it grows. Should the organization chart be wide and flat, tall and hierarchical, or some combination of the two?

Many startup founders romanticize the idea of a collaborative, egalitarian work environment. They cherish the idea of abandoning hierarchy and working together in harmony.

In companies with deep organizational hierarchies, political maneuvering and competition can emerge as employees struggle to move up the ladder. People who are lower in the hierarchy are less likely to take risks. They may feel that it's not their place to speak up, or that they have limited ability to move up in the future with a static organization above them.

A "flat" organizational structure holds a special appeal for companies that depend on innovation and risk taking, like startups. Successful startups develop a culture that embraces failure and encourages experimentation.

Despite the pull toward less structure and hierarchy, organizational structure plays an important role for fast-growing startups. Decision-making under pressure requires clearly delineated roles and accountability.

Collaboration doesn't mean an absence of structure.

A startup cannot overcome the formidable challenge of rapid growth without clear roles and responsibilities.

Research shows that organizational hierarchies improve performance when two factors are present: competent leadership and employees who are empowered to fulfill their responsibilities. For startups, the optimal organizational structure may be broad with few hierarchical layers in which people have clearly defined authority and roles. Ideal leadership and team practices for a startup includes:

- Adaptive leadership (the hippo mentioned in the previous chapter) that steps in when necessary but gives others room to take risks and learn

- A team and corporate culture that embraces learning from failures

- Diverse teams with differentiated skill sets

- Clearly defined roles and understanding of what each team member brings to the team

Create an attitude of equality that empowers individual contributors, while clearly defining decision-making authority and responsibilities.

ROLES AND RESPONSIBILITIES

Startup teams often work best when each individual on the team has a clear understanding of his or her responsibilities. Defining those roles is one of the first startup hurdles. Execution often falters when there are unspoken assumptions about ownership and accountability.

Manned space missions involve life-threatening situations that require fast decision-making. According to Larry W. Keyser, an assistant flight director on Apollo 13:

> *The lack of immediate action, when required, because of undefined responsibilities or authority, can be just as disastrous as the wrong action.*

Startups live in a world of time-critical situations, always in danger of burning too much fuel or going off-course. Lack of clarity about roles and decision-making authority hampers decisiveness. Many startups struggle with questions about how to divide responsibilities and authority.

Clearly defined roles and decision-making authority foster accountability and collaboration. One vehicle for defining roles is the DACI model. DACI is an acronym for four key areas of responsibility:

- **DRIVER:** The driver is accountable for moving a project forward. One individual fills this role for each area of the business or major project. As is the case with an automobile, you don't want two drivers piloting the vehicle.

- **APPROVER:** People in this role sign off on the project and approve major changes. This is often the person at the top of a business unit, department, or company who also wields veto (the "no-go") power. In a startup, the CEO often fills the Approver role.

- **CONTRIBUTOR:** Individuals may contribute to multiple projects and business areas. Teams work best when contributors are acknowledged and know exactly what is expected of them.

- **INFORMED:** People in this role are kept informed about status updates and significant changes, but are not called on to make decisions and don't expect their opinion to carry weight in the decision-making process.

You may not want to use a structured approach like the DACI model for every decision area. But for important business initiatives or controversial projects, a clear definition of roles and expectations will streamline decision-making, increase alignment, and reduce internal conflict.

AREAS AND RESPONSIBILITIES

Startup Fictiv uses a system called Areas of Responsibility and Key Results to assign roles and decision-making authority. Individuals on the team each operate within a clearly defined scope of responsibility and identify their own key results, which are specific, measurable goals that people meet to contribute to business objectives.

The entire team holds each team member responsible for the results in their area. Within each area, final decision authority rests with the person who owns the responsibility—usually the person who knows the most about it. As founder and CEO, Dave Evans sees his role as removing roadblocks so that each team member can operate effectively within an individual area of responsibility.

What happens when an employee makes a decision the CEO does not agree with? According to Evans, "As CEO, of course, I have veto power over almost any important decision, but I rarely need to use it." Having put the team in place, he empowers them to take responsibility.

MISSION RULES FOR STARTUPS

Build the Company You Want to Run

Every aspect of the astronaut's daily environment in space was carefully designed and engineered, from the living quarters to the spacesuits the astronauts wore and the food they ate. Successful execution under pressure depends on careful advanced planning.

Startup leaders have the opportunity to design the company's working environment before it reaches a critical mass. Even with a brilliant idea and the ideal founding team, success ultimately relies on execution. Execution depends, in part, on how you shape the environment for team members and how that environment evolves as the team grows.

As an entrepreneur, you are not just building a product or service—you're building a business. Put the same care into the architecture of the organization as the design of the solution you're selling. The early foundations support the business that you plan to become.

INTENTIONAL CREATION OF VALUES AND CULTURE

The previous chapter discussed the importance of building diverse teams with complementary skills and talents. Cross-functional teams work together well when they share common values. One of the first tasks of the startup launch team is to identify and agree on those values, then to design a work environment that supports them.

Values are established by leaders and founders;
culture is shaped by day-to-day interactions.

Your company's values may be closely related to your solution, or how you work with each other and customers. They may also encompass the impact that your business hopes to have on the world at large.

A business is never too small to define its values. San Francisco–based startup Fictiv offers online tools for hardware engineers to order parts from a network of 3-D printers and hardware manufacturers, enabling better lead times and prices for engineers, while helping vendors improve the utilization of their printers. As the founder of the manufacturing startup and survivor of past startups, Dave Evans realizes the importance of values.

He took his 10-person team—the entire staff of the company at the time—to an off-site meeting to create a values document for the young and growing company. As a self-described community of makers, tinkers, and hobbyists, the team came up with values such as respect for diversity, support for innovation, and individual empowerment. These values align well with the company's core customer base of hardware designers.

Says Evans, "The culture you create as a company is reflected in the product you deliver and the impact your organization makes in the world."

But establishing values is only the first step. Ultimately, workplace culture is shaped by what happens every day, without structure or planning. By engineering the day-to-day environment and culture with intention, you create a business in which the culture reflects the values of founders and employees. Without an alignment of culture and values, workplaces often become conflict-ridden.

If you don't define the culture, the culture
will define itself, for better or worse.

One well-funded and fast-growing startup in San Francisco was in discussions for acquisition by an ideal, market-leading suitor. The negotiations fell apart during due diligence when the acquiring company discovered a problem with their accidental culture. The decision-making process was intractably broken. When the acquiring company requested business plans and financial documents, the company took weeks to produce them. They discovered that the delay was due to the fact that all decisions at the company flowed through the founder, who had become a critical bottleneck. As a result, the company lacked the muscles of distributed decision-making and delegation, which would be critical for it to scale and deal with the competitive market environment. The acquiring company killed the deal.

In her research into conflict in startups, Lindy Greer of the Stanford Graduate School of Business has discovered that startup founders who lack awareness of their vision and values often fail to intentionally shape the culture, and this can be a huge problem down the road. She tells us that in her experience, "Founders who are on their third startup onward tend to be much more intentional and explicit about leadership and decision-making in a way that first-time entrepreneurs almost never are. Most startups fail because of people problems. By their second or third startup, founders are better at the people stuff, and intentionally create the right hierarchy and culture for the company."

Entrepreneurs who have lived through one or more startups often spend time focusing on culture at the beginning because they know the importance of this intangible quality to their success. First-time entrepreneurs may lack sufficient experience in varying workplaces to gain insight into what is unique about their environment and the importance of culture in business.

Beyond agreeing on values, startup founders can shape the work environment and culture in a way that best supports the unique requirements of a startup by being intentional in the design of the physical environment, the culture, and the rules of engagement.

DESIGN THE CREW QUARTERS

Where will people work? What will the office space look like, and how will you fill it?

Necessity, convenience, and budget often dictate early workplace decisions. Businesses are launched in garages, startup incubators, and dorm rooms. Perhaps there's an affordable office space near the founder's home. No matter where you land, configure the environment to support the way you plan to work together, even when bound by resource and space constraints.

Physical location affects human interactions. People make stronger connections when co-located because they can communicate using body language as well as words. Even if people work remotely, arrange face-to-face meetings to strengthen personal relationships.

Office configuration affects work styles and workflows. People read status and importance into physical location, whether proximity to windows, size of office, or other factors. Physical barriers like walls can easily become organizational barriers. For this reason, many startups adopt an open floor plan, with banks of desks.

Location contributes to creativity and serendipitous interactions. When building Pixar's Emeryville, Calif., headquarters, Steve Jobs sought to design a space that encouraged collaboration and creativity. The building design influences traffic flow so that people from diverse groups meet and interact during the day. With a giant atrium space and centralized restrooms, the space facilitates unplanned encounters. Whimsical statues from Pixar films inspire and remind people of the legacy they are inheriting and advancing. The space itself fosters a sense of creative play.

TRY THE STRATEGIC SEATING SHIFT

Lee Caraher, CEO of the San Francisco–based public relations and digital marketing firm Double Forte, alters the seating plan for her team every few months. Each time, she locates team members from the most critical business area next to her desk in the open floor plan. When the firm launched a major initiative to transform its client base, the person in charge of business development sat at the desk next to the Caraher. Whoever sits in the "hot seat" next to the CEO gets extra attention, and that drives close communication and better results.

Develop a Culture of Risk Taking and Learning

Just as startup leaders benefit from a learning orientation, startups must be agile and open to the lessons of the market, adjusting course as needed. Successful startups learn and adapt as an organization.

The best startup environments embrace risk taking and tolerate failure.

The organizational structure and leadership style can either stifle or promote innovation. To create a culture of innovation, startup leaders couple processes and structures that support and encourage risk taking with practices that foster learning.

66 There was a tremendous feeling of openness among our organizations. We grew up telling each other we were making mistakes when we made them. And that is how we learned. 99

CHRISTOPHER KRAFT,
director of Flight Operations for the Apollo program,
later director of the Johnson Space Center

For example, developers at an online marketplace for hotel booking regularly test how consumers will respond to new design options for their website by using "sandbox" environments. Online businesses can do this effectively because with high usage, they can generate rich data and perform side-by-side experiments in real time. While the company's CEO expects that a majority of the experiments will fail, he knows that the one or two that succeed are critical to drive innovation.

By focusing on learning from results and data, the company creates an environment in which experimentation is not only encouraged, but expected. The words you choose to encourage innovation matter. One startup we work with intentionally describes projects and initiatives as *experiments*. Why? The concept of an experiment establishes an expectation of both positive and negative results. Risking failure is an expected part of the learning process.

ENGINEER ATTENTION IN THE
DAY-TO-DAY ENVIRONMENT

The urgent demands of day-to-day business often divert our attention from what's important, particularly in the fast-paced startup environment.

Although everyone may agree with stated shared values, it's essential to create an environment that actively supports those values as the company expands and daily challenges accelerate.

Our focus and attention drive our actions.

How often have you heard a company claim to be "customer-centric," yet then fail miserably in customer service? It's easy to lose focus on the customer when the customer is absent from the work environment.

As a cloud-based solution for building and testing landing pages, Unbounce is strongly committed to customer success. The Customer Success team created a video dashboard to display customer survey data and comments so team members can see what is happening with customers in real time. According to VP of Customer Success Ryan Engley, "The dashboards were set up by the main entrance, so as everyone came and went, the entire company would see them. People often stop to ask questions and have conversations." When moving to new headquarters, the company installed the dashboard in a common area so the voice of the customer remained visible to everyone. Many businesses claim to be customer-focused; Unbounce *designs* the customer focus into the physical workplace.

How you engineer attention in the workplace will depend on your business and values. Here are a few stories for inspiration.

Employees at The Webby Awards each have a small bell on their desk—a little chiming bell like the one used at the front desk of a motel. Employees ring the bell whenever something positive happens, drawing attention to success. While this practice might be annoying in another environment, at The Webby Awards it reinforces an attitude of celebration and sharing success with others, and aligns perfectly with an organization that honors excellence on the Internet.

At manufacturing startup Fictiv, the office is filled with the products built by employees. People sit at handmade desks. The team designed and built their own doorbell hardware with a 3-D printer, and coded it to play a custom tune, composed by a musical employee. The projects scattered around the office align with the values and culture of people who love to tinker, collaborate, and invent things—attributes of the company's customers, hardware designers. The physical workplace draws attention to the core mission of the business.

At legal search startup Judicata, employees answer questions from state bar review courses over shared lunches. The practice began when an engineer questioned aloud whether he could pass the state bar exam. The team decided to answer that question by bringing in bar review questions. What started as a fun challenge has turned into a shared tradition, anchored by a meal, that keeps employees focused on the interests and domain of its customers—the law.

Now the team answers bar questions with interview candidates and with investors and advisors when they visit the office. They are particularly impressed by one of their investors who has never missed a question.

SHARE A MEAL

A growing number of companies provide their employees with lunches. In addition to being a valuable recruiting tool, the activity of eating together can cement team relationships. At many businesses, communal dining facilities are where people interact with others outside of their direct teams.

Researchers led by applied behavioral scientist Kevin Kniffin of Cornell University have found that firefighting teams that eat meals together cooperate better on the job.

In the early days of Box, lunch was the one time that everyone on the founding team was present. The team would order takeout lunch and send someone to pick it up. These informal lunches provided great conversations and built valuable connections between team members. As the company grew, the ritual evolved into a Friday employee lunch program that serves to bring everyone in the company together.

EMBRACE AND MANAGE CONFLICT

Every entrepreneur dreams of building a cohesive team that works together well, without conflict. While conflicts can lead to startup failures, conflict itself isn't the problem. Research suggests that conflict is actually an essential element for startup success.

In his book *The Myths of Creativity*, author David Burkus debunks the idea that creativity only flourishes when criticism and conflict are absent. According to Burkus, "Just below the surface of many outstanding creative teams, you'll find that their process relies on structured conflict, not cohesion."

Defending your ideas, anticipating criticism, and building on the insights of others makes for better ideas. Most innovations emerge from the efforts of multiple contributors.

Constructive conflict fuels moonshots.

One way to integrate healthy conflict is to assign and rotate the role of devil's advocate among team members. Playing this role hones the ability to deliver constructive criticism, without negativity or personal attack. This person has the explicit responsibility to point out potential issues and problems. Research shows that having a devil's advocate on the team improves creativity, decisions, and outcomes—but only when the dissenting opinions are presented in a non-confrontational way.

Conflict can be either productive or toxic. Productive conflict advances the work. Toxic conflict interferes with team productivity and people's ability to work together.

At Pixar, a veritable hotbed of creativity, every frame of film is subject to intense criticism in daily reviews. When offering a critique, people also offer a suggestion for improving the issue cited in the film. This keeps the focus of the discussion on the work, not the individuals.

Conflict is damaging when it is about personalities and power rather than the work. Personal conflicts and power struggles that derail startups appear during the stresses of rapid growth.

Having researched conflict in startup teams, Lindy Greer tells us that arguments over process and logistics are often the most damaging types of negative conflict—even worse than open personality clashes, because they represent personal conflict that is disguised as a work issue. Process conflicts frequently veil struggles over other issues, such as status or respect.

Effective conflict is work related, not personal.

To avoid toxic conflict, make sure you're discussing the real issue and that those issues are business issues, not personal ones. Focusing on data and results is critical. Says Dave Evans at Fictiv, "When there are dissents, we have brutally honest conversations. We're experimental and data-driven, so people lay it all out on the table."

Practices for Avoiding Toxic Conflict

- Clearly define roles and responsibilities; understand who has the ultimate decision authority.

- Define how you will manage conflict and disagreements in a Rules of Engagement pledge.

- Encourage frankness and facilitate discussion of difficult issues.

- Assign the devil's advocate role to an individual with a high degree of emotional intelligence on a team; rotate the position if multiple people are capable of filling it.

WRITE YOUR RULES OF ENGAGEMENT

The chapter "Cultivating a High-Performing Team" describes the practice of creating an explicit Rules of Engagement pledge for how teams will interact while engaged in a moonshot. The basic Rules of Engagement might include commitments such as acknowledging others' contributions, being on time and responsive, acknowledging problems, and engaging with respect.

In a startup, the Rules of Engagement may cover a different set of issues. Having read this chapter, work with your team to identify the values and culture you want to create, and design pledges that support those values. For example:

- I am an advocate for the company when interacting with others outside the business.

- I agree to behave in a way that is consistent with company values.

- I will ask for assistance when needed or when I see that a milestone is in danger.

- I commit to only calling meetings with a clear and specific purpose, and adhering to the rules of effective meetings.

- I will not avoid difficult conversations or constructive conflict. When I have a problem or disagreement with someone, I will keep the discussion focused on the business issue.

- I will welcome constructive criticism for my own ideas and initiatives, and put the needs of the business ahead of my personal need for glory.

- Whenever possible, I will pair a criticism or negative evaluation with a suggestion for improvement.

CHAPTER 28

STARTUP STORIES

The Entrepreneur as Storyteller

As your business grows and people join, how do you keep every-one working toward the same vision? How do you sustain the environment that you have carefully crafted?

Turn to a proven, powerful instrument for aligning vision and culture: story.

Since the dawn of time, people have used stories to transmit cultural values. In today's world of information overload, the ancient art of story-telling is even more critical. Stories can reinforce important values in your business, convince others to join you on your mission, and bring new hires onboard who are aligned with the broader mission.

Storytelling is essential for the startup entrepreneur.

As your company grows, stories shape the business narrative, having employees and customers alike understand how you work together and what you are working toward.

A successful startup generates many kinds of stories, including:

- Founding stories

- War stories

- Values stories

- Customer stories

Collect and curate stories to strengthen your business and team dynamics.

FOUNDING STORIES

Every startup has a founding story. The best founding stories illustrate something about the business itself. For example:

- Founded by climber Yves Chouinard, Patagonia was built on the principle of deep respect for the environment. That attitude continues to this day.

- Apple's co-founders Steve Jobs and Steve Wozniak filled the roles of the creative designer and the practical engineer. Apple's corporate identity remains closely allied with the marriage of superior design and technical excellence.

The founding story may be an important part of your pitch for funding, so it's worth the time to get it right.

While data and business plans appeal to investors' rational minds, story speaks to a more powerful and primal part of the brain. If you want people to remember you, tell a good story. Venture capital investor Lisa Suennen emphasizes the importance of storytelling for startups: "Entrepreneurs' inability to tell a compelling story may well be the number one barrier to success in getting venture funding."

President Kennedy didn't talk about sending rockets and landing vehicles to the moon; he crafted a human story about sending people to the moon and bringing them safely home.

VALUES STORIES

While many businesses *claim* values, statements of values are often abstract and difficult to internalize. (What does "Don't be evil." really mean?) Vaguely defined values are easily overrun by business-as-usual demands. Too often, no one beyond the founders can remember the business's stated values.

Stories put values into context in meaningful and memorable ways. Stories that illustrate values may include:

- Hypothetical scenarios: These stories illustrate how your values apply in difficult situations. For example: *We claim to care about customer service; would we accept used shoes for return?*

- Actual stories: Examples of difficult decisions based on stated values.

When values are expressed through stories, they take on new life.

Some companies articulate their values and stories in a doctrine or manifesto. Famous examples include:

- The HP Way—a framework of five principles set out by Bill Hewlett and David Packard.

- The Zen of Palm—a manifesto of design philosophies and design principles for designing for Palm, Inc.

- Facebook and the Hacker Way—a culture and management approach that Facebook shares with all new employees. When filing the prospectus for its Initial Public Offering, Facebook CEO Mark Zuckerberg described the manifesto in a letter to prospective investors.

Ritz-Carlton actively trains employees on the company's service values, such as being responsive to the expressed and unexpressed wishes of customers, or owning and resolving customer problems. Ritz employees start the day with a 15-minute standing meeting called the daily lineup. In it, managers make announcements and share stories to illustrate the Ritz Gold Standards, core values of the organization.

The Ritz-Carlton website collects and share stories of employees at various properties that embody and demonstrate these values through exceptional service. Examples include chefs that visited a bride's grandmother in advance of the wedding so they could prepare Russian fare using authentic recipes, or extraordinary efforts to launch last-minute wedding ceremonies in blizzards. The company shares these stories on its customer-facing website, in the section "Stories That Stay With You." More importantly, employees hear these stories in the daily lineup, a practice often used in high-end restaurants to prepare the staff before service begins, to inspire and promote exceptional service at all levels.

WAR STORIES

In the minutes before landing on the moon, Neil Armstrong noticed that the automated navigation system was about to set the landing craft down in the middle of a boulder-filled crater. He took control of the lunar module and steered it instead to a flat area, landing 6 kilometers from the programmed site with just enough fuel to spare. As previously mentioned, the lunar Sea of Tranquility, up close, wasn't as tranquil as it seemed. The path of a young business is similarly strewn with potential boulders. Every startup generates war stories of the adventures that the employees go through together. These stories trace the growth of the company and the shared experiences while illustrating the progress made so far.

- "Remember when we had to use the outlet in the men's room to shrink-wrap the product boxes?"

- "Remember when we didn't have a meeting room and interviewed every new candidate in the local coffee shop?"

- "Remember the first six months, when the founders slept in the conference room because they didn't want to go home? Remember the engineers who slept in sleeping bags under their desks?"

Collect those stories; they represent the company history and strengthen ties between employees. Share them to reinforce founding values as the company grows.

The best stories profile heroic action or illuminate the personalities of key players in the business. Select stories that define the business *as you want it to be*. The stories you share will shape the business environment of your future.

CUSTOMER STORIES

When pitching to customers, you tell another type of story.

In this story, the *customer* is the hero engaged on an epic journey; your solution aids the hero's journey. Whether you're pitching the value proposition to prospective customers or sharing the story of an early adopter, remember to make the customer the hero.

For inspiring examples of this kind of empowerment marketing, look to the Adidas #mygirls campaign, which originated in 2013. The company shares stories of young women achieving remarkable things in sports. More recently, Proctor & Gamble's Always brands invites young women to share their stories of smashing limitations with its #LikeAGirl campaign. In both cases, the customers are the heroes of the stories; the brands themselves support and empower those heroes.

STORYTELLING PRACTICES

As you collect and practice telling stories, remember the basic rules of storytelling.

STORY STRUCTURE: A simple story has three components: beginning, middle, and end. When constructing a compelling story, consider using an expanded structure, called Freytag's Pyramid, after the nineteenth-century novelist and playwright who analyzed hundreds of stories in search of shared patterns. He came up with the following basic story structure as being nearly universal:

1. **Exposition—setting the scene**

2. **Inciting moment—action begins**

3. **Rising action—the story builds**

4. **Climax**—the moment of greatest tension

5. **Falling action**—what happens as a result of the climax

6. **Resolution**—the main problem or conflict is solved

7. **Denouement**—the ending; remaining secrets or questions are answered

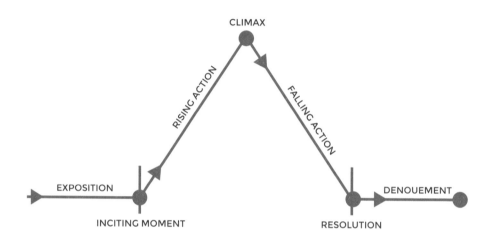

To turn a real-world anecdote into a compelling story, trim and fit the details to the key elements: exposition, inciting moment (when something begins the action), climax of the conflict, resolution, and denouement. Use concrete detail where possible to enhance credibility.

CONCRETE DETAILS: One challenge of telling a good story is getting the right amount of information, striking the balance between sufficient detail and rambling. Include enough concrete detail to make the story interesting and real, but not so much that you overwhelm the main objective of the story.

THE RIGHT HERO: The hero of the story is *not* the one telling the story; that's bragging. In customer stories, customers are heroes. In the business stories, heroes include the employees or investors. Your *brand* is never the hero. Instead, it's something that aids other heroes on their journeys.

Invite New Employees Into the Stories

How do you keep the stories going during times of rapid growth? Use stories to share the company history.

One startup we work with gives recruits a "history lesson" using stories. At Facebook, new employees receive a book containing stories that illustrate the Hacker Way culture as part of orientation. Culture is part of the six-week Facebook Engineering Bootcamp that every new engineering employee at Facebook attends, whether a recent grad or new director. During bootcamp, engineers learn about the many opportunities at the company so they can join teams for projects they are passionate about. Participants form bonds with co-workers that persist, facilitating cross-team communication. The bootcamp is not just about code, it's also about culture.

Culture is shared and reinforced through story. Through stories, new hires can take their place in the same narrative as those who are already there.

IN-FLIGHT OPERATIONS

Stay on Course

On every Apollo flight, ground controllers carefully plotted the spacecraft's progress on its flight path, sending minor course corrections during the flight. The crew always knew exactly where they were, how much fuel was left, and what their options were. The objective of the mission was clear.

Startups require a similar focus. Everyone involved in a startup expects to be crazy busy, but effort alone isn't enough.

Success isn't about activity, it's about results.

Success demands that leaders create milestones and engineer completions.

Entrepreneurs often struggle to keep the team aligned while executing pre-determined milestones and objectives. Even as they shift and pivot in response to changing conditions and customer feedback, the best leaders maintain a steadfast focus on where they are going.

This chapter covers strategies for maintaining alignment to your most important objectives.

CREATE 30-DAY MILESTONES AND 90-DAY COMPLETIONS

Startups exist in a constant state of tension between this week's urgent tasks and what must happen to support the business three, six, or twelve months in the future.

Many startups, particularly early stage, operate in an insular way. Executives in larger, established companies struggle with urgent external demands from competitors and customers. Startup leaders are not burdened with external demands when their products and services are not yet out in the marketplace. Instead, they must sift through the clutter of ideas to determine what is essential to the business.

One way to cut through the clutter and focus on what matters most is to add 30-day objectives and 90-day milestones to planning processes. Ninety days is long enough to achieve meaningful milestones, while 30-day interim objectives maintain a tight focus.

We recommend that startup teams focus on no more than three key objectives in a 30-day period, and renew these objectives every 30 days. If one of the three objectives gets completed within the window, add another.

When you reach the end of the 90-day time frame, which may coincide with a calendar quarter, stop and mark its completion. Then recommit to the next 90-day milestone. Burnout is endemic to startups; observing completions is one way to alleviate burnout. To this end, consider implementing the following ideas:

- Use a completion event to process and internalize what you've learned so far, reinforcing the culture of learning and experimentation.

- Acknowledge the efforts that have brought you to this point. Acknowledgment is vital in startups, where participants often move forward with heroic efforts.

- Completions can reengage and revitalize a team with renewed energy and focus.

WORK BACKWARD FROM CRITICAL MILESTONES

How do you choose the 30-day milestones? Work backward from critical long-term objectives.

Milestones shift; that's a fact of startup life. Decision-making becomes easier when everyone is aligned around the most important milestones and understands their dependencies and interconnections.

The CEO of Judicata targeted a release date six months out for the next funding round. He assembled the management team to map out exactly what they had to do to secure funding within six months. The team identified explicit, calendar-based milestones to achieve that objective, including:

- Customer acquisition targets

- Usage metrics

- Product release schedules

A few weeks before the proposed release date, a manager on the product team uncovered a major data problem with the product, which put the feature-complete release date in jeopardy. Because she had been part of the team creating the road map to the funding milestone, she understood an important fact: the funding depended on the product release date. Slipping this date imperiled the company's fuel supply.

She asked the team to make an extraordinary effort, working together through a weekend to resolve the problem with the data. The entire team agreed to work over the weekend, and others not on the team volunteered to join in their effort because they all understood the importance of the objective. The effort wasn't about meeting an arbitrary deadline; it was critical to the company's financial well-being and survival. Everyone was aligned toward the common goal.

USE ON-TRACK/OFF-TRACK REPORTING

When you're engaged in tight time frames, use quick status meetings with the on-track/off-track formula.

On-track or off-track reporting delivers a binary yes or no answer based solely on facts. Reporting in this way shifts the focus from activity to result. In these meetings, the meeting leader asks one question: "Are you on track or off track?"

When a team member answers, the next question is "How do you know?" Listen for fact-based evidence that maps to their key milestones. People often confuse activity with results, and this question is designed to ensure they report on results.

Then ask about the upcoming milestone: "What will you accomplish by the next meeting in order to stay on track?"

When someone reports being off track, ask the person for a plan *with a timeline* to get back on track.

Here's how on-track or off-track reporting sounds:

The head of design says: "We are on track. By last Friday our target was to have acquired 500 users for our beta. We hit 526 last Friday so we are on track. By our next meeting in two weeks, or goal is to have acquired a total of 1,000 users, and with our current outreach plans we will meet or exceed that goal."

MAKE CLEAR REQUESTS

During the journey to the moon's surface and back, essential data transmission was intermittent. Voice communications were lost during portions of the flight behind the moon, and during reentry, and often garbled during handoffs between different stations on Earth. No one took communication for granted.

Mission Control issued explicit requests and precise instructions. Crew members acknowledged and answered requests promptly, and described conditions or anomalies clearly. Personal conversation and connections happened after vital business was concluded. Because the communication medium was uncertain, people made the best use of the bandwidth, getting the important information across as quickly as possible.

Startups similarly demand concise and immediate transmissions of information. Requests turn ideas into action. That's why it's critical to make clear requests.

The chapter "The Art of Requests" outlines the elements of a well-formed request. To summarize, complete requests include the following components:

1. **THE REQUESTOR AND REQUESTEE:** Identify the person doing the asking and the specific individual asked to undertake something.

2. **SPECIFIC, OUTCOME-BASED REQUIREMENTS:** Be clear about the desired outcome; leave the details of execution to the requestee.

3. **CALENDAR-READY TIME FRAME:** Include a specific deadline to eliminate any ambiguity.

Turn requests into commitment and action by doing the following after making the request:

- **Confirm the commitment:** Did you hear yes, no, or a counteroffer?

- **Follow-up:** Agree on when and where you'll follow up on the request.

The lack of clear, specific requests frequently derails startups, and the results can be damaging.

As an example, a company we worked with was in the beta testing phase of its software product. The product marketing team gathered and consolidated feedback from the beta customers and posted it to an internal wiki—a collaborative, online environment for sharing information. The engineering team regularly reviewed the wiki and implemented changes to the product.

Thirty days before the scheduled launch, the product marketing and engineering teams met to review the requirements for the final release. They discovered that they could not implement two of the most critical changes in time to meet the product launch deadline.

Although the two teams regularly met and reviewed the beta test data, specific requests were unspoken. The online collaboration platform gave people a false sense of security about their actual communication and collaboration. The product marketing lead had not specifically identified the most critical implementation changes, nor had the engineering lead indicated the calendar-ready deadline by which they needed the requirements list. The lack of clear, specific requests doomed the launch deadline.

This issue could have been avoided had the engineering lead made an effective request of product marketing. For example:

"I ask that you, Helen (head of product marketing), deliver a prioritized list of bug fixes and enhancements for the next release by February 17 at 5 p.m. We will review the changes and respond by February 19 at 5 p.m. with what we can implement in time for the launch."

CHAPTER 30

CALL IN THE ROCKET SCIENTISTS

Ask for Advice

Isaac Newton claimed that as a scientist, he stood on the shoulders of the giants who had gone before him. Startups accelerate when they find as many shoulders as possible to stand on. Expertise from outside the organization is critical, even when breaking fresh ground and disrupting industries.

Many startup leaders don't seek enough outside advice. The pull of gravity is to craft solutions entirely from within their own teams. As a result, when they hit a wall, they don't have experts on hand to engineer a breakthrough.

There's a name for this situation: "Not Invented Here." The term describes the tendency to overlook or actively reject superior solutions that originate outside the business. Organizations that exhibit Not Invented Here tendencies attempt to engineer and optimize every part of their solution on their own.

If you create everything in-house, you'll reinvent a thousand wheels. As a startup, you don't have time for that while operating on a short runway. Although you might generate excellent solutions to tricky problems, focusing solely within consumes a great deal of time and energy when your startup has limited fuel to stay aloft.

Using outside experts and advice accelerates your journey by identifying proven pathways and known solutions so you can avoid costly and time-consuming detours.

FIND YOUR ADVISORS

Around every startup, dozens of people are ready to step forward and offer advice. These may include:

- Board members

- Investors

- Clients and customers

- Experts

- Friends and former colleagues

- Advisory board members

- Coaches and mentors

These existing network contacts can provide powerful assistance. But don't stop there. Reach outside the usual circles to identify people with relevant perspectives that can save you trouble down the road.

As your startup grows, look for other advisors to offer guidance. Here are some questions to start building out your network of advisors.

- Who is publishing research related to your business?

- Can your board members recommend potential advisors?

- Who are the thought leaders in your industry?

- Who outside your industry may have solved similar problems or faced similar challenges?

Lindy Greer, a professor at the Stanford Graduate School of Business, highlights the importance of first-time founders seeking advisors, mentors, and coaches: "Startup founders are often worse at leadership than they realize. The entrepreneurs who fail typically don't have strong networks and coaches, and do not seek advice. Entrepreneurs with a learning mentality are the exception, and it's a powerful advantage."

ASK FOR ADVICE BEFORE YOU NEED IT

Having assembled your team of advisors, how do you engage them to get the most value from their expertise?

You could wait for a crisis. Asking for outside advice is one strategy for getting to a breakthrough. But it's much more effective to ask for advice regularly, as an intentional practice. If you wait until you have a specific problem to ask for advice, you'll only get answers to questions you know to ask.

Engage advisors before you need them. Connect with advisors intentionally and consistently to expand their value. You will broaden your perspective, and may also discover possibilities or prevent problems before they happen. By asking, you only commit to *listen*, not to *act*. You cannot realistically act on all the advice you receive. Processing and prioritizing it makes you smarter, and may make your business run more smoothly.

When Aaron Levie reached out to industry leaders while building Box, he made a simple, direct request of each: to have coffee. Many people did, and became long-term supporters and advisors. He listened to and learned from all of them. When Tom Siebel of Siebel Systems and Craig Conway of PeopleSoft told Levie he was not spending enough time with customers, he started meeting with eight customers per week, asking questions about what worked and what didn't.

Customers can make great advisors, too.

WORK THE ADVISORY BOARD

Having the right industry pundits on your board of directors and advisory board creates essential social proof for your company. Many startups stockpile advisors on their advisory boards to earn important bragging rights.

Having populated advisory boards with luminaries, a surprising number of startups fail to take advantage of them. Don't waste these connections.

Don't assume that advisors will pick up the phone or proactively reach out with sage words of wisdom at the right moment. They won't. Waiting for people to contact you with advice is unrealistic. Everyone is busy. Your advisors are not aware of the issues you're struggling with; they might not even remember exactly what you're doing. The daily issues of your business aren't as high a priority for them as they are for you.

Waiting for a crisis limits the value of your board. We recommend that you schedule regular contact with advisors, both individually and as a group:

- At least once a month, connect with someone from your advisor network for input.

- Ideally, connect with each advisor on your list at least quarterly.

This may sound daunting, but the actual interactions can be brief and simple:

- "Here's what we're doing with our new features."

- "These are some of the issues we're working on right now."

- "Our customers are asking about this . . . what are your thoughts?"

- "What questions should I be asking in our business that I may not be asking?"

- "What questions could I be asking you that I haven't asked?"

Schedule these conversations in your calendar and make them happen.

BRING ADVISORS TOGETHER

In addition to individual meetings, many startup founders invite advisors to assemble as a group once or twice a year. When people gather together, their interactions change. Good ideas feed off each other, and different individuals offer unique perspectives on each other's advice.

Arranging annual meetings requires you to set aside time to meet and prepare materials. These advisory board meetings have many benefits, including the following:

- Regular meetings keep your business concerns fresh in advisors' minds, making it more likely that they will offer relevant insight.

- In-person meetings expose leaders within your team to key advisors, potentially strengthening the team's expertise and industry standing.

- Preparing for the meeting requires that you take stock of what you've accomplished and think deeply about the challenges ahead.

REPORT TO GROUND CONTROL

Managing Your Boards and Investors

The board of directors may be a formality in the early days of your business, but over time, the importance of the board grows. Particularly when investors hold key seats, the board may become a lifeline, the ground control for your mission. The farther you go on your mission, the more important communications with the board become.

To manage growth, you'll need to work well with your board.

In the early days of a startup, board meetings may be informal. Early board members may focus on providing financial guidance and big-picture ideas. The board may also be useful in finding the right team members to fuel growth.

As your business grows, so does the role and impact of the board. As you progress through funding rounds, investors may join your board, contributing their expertise and applying their own perspectives to your business issues. As the business matures, board guidance often becomes more focused as the board fills the role of a fiduciary representative for other investors.

This chapter covers practices for maintaining good relationships with individual board members and the board as a whole.

KNOW THE DRILL

No matter the size of your board, you must adhere to certain rules. Boards play well-defined roles. Board minutes serve as a critical record of decisions and board approvals of important issues including stock allocation, stock option pricing, and approval to hire executives and raise money. If you're not familiar with the requirements to document board meetings, find someone who does, such as your corporate lawyer, and ask them to attend. Make sure you understand which decisions in the business require board approval, and which you can make autonomously.

Board meetings require preparation; most boards request that meeting materials be sent several days in advance of the date. Time is precious for everyone, and running a disorganized meeting simply wastes time at a larger scale.

Start the meeting by reminding the board of the commitments and decisions you made at the previous meeting. Update them on what you have done since that time, and how that compares to what you promised in the last meeting. Then make sure they know about any problems or issues you're facing, what you're doing about them, and make requests for any guidance you are seeking.

Be clear in requesting advice or decisions; differentiate between a status update and a request for a decision. Before leaving, also clarify the timing and commitments for the next board meeting.

As you participate in a board meeting, the seven key rules of Communicating Up apply:

1. Be concise and lead with the summary. Have the details ready on request.

2. Speak clearly and plainly. Ditch the jargon and frame the discussion in terms everyone can understand.

3. Be relevant. Focus on the board members' perspective, which may be broader than your daily concerns. Frame the discussion based on their priorities and objectives.

4. Be bold. Take a stand and make recommendations.

5. Be specific in requests. Know what you want to ask from the board and request it explicitly.

6. Reframe results as possibilities. Focus on the possibilities that results will open up; elevate the discussion and look ahead.

7. Be consistent. Set expectations for the next communications, and then stick to your schedule consistently.

For some startups, it's worth adding an eighth rule: Wear shoes when meeting with the board. We work in Silicon Valley; this needs to be said.

Sample Board Meeting Agenda

Use the following framework to organize and run board meetings:

- What commitments we made at the last board meeting

- What we accomplished

- Problems or issues we'd like to make the board aware of and get input on

- Decisions and actions the board needs to take

- Date and time of next board meeting

- Commitments for next board meeting

MAINTAIN INDIVIDUAL RELATIONSHIPS

During every board meeting, the investors on your board are asking themselves these questions: "Are you the best CEO for this company? Is the current leadership the right team to lead the company forward?"

The board's responsibility is to the company, not to you personally. Don't give board members an excuse to decide you're not up to the task of CEO.

If you have difficult news to convey, communicate it before the meeting, in individual phone calls to key board members. You know the saying about "absence makes the heart grow fonder"? That doesn't hold true for board members and investors in your business. For investors, the absence of communication may be grounds for worry.

Board members and advisors can become your biggest allies when you communicate regularly and effectively, and provide pathways for them to contribute to the success of your business.

PART FIVE

Reentry

I f you've read sequentially to this point, you've completed the book. But a completion isn't necessarily an ending. Let's take a moment to reflect on this landing—and your next steps.

When the Apollo 11 astronauts returned to Earth, they were scrubbed down with iodine to prevent contamination, and then quarantined.

Don't do that.

We encourage you to do the opposite: go ahead and "contaminate" others with what you've learned. Share the useful tools and practices with your colleagues. If you're on a team, share the habits of high-performing teams, and see what happens.

We've structured the book as a useful reference guide that you can return to as often as needed. Use the book when you step into a new role or undertake a new moonshot.

If you're like most of the people we work with, once you've completed one moonshot, you'll want to come back for more. You may find ways to apply the principles of the moonshot, and harvest its effects, in multiple positions or even different aspects of your life.

So rather than calling this an ending, let's say it's a milestone completion. Here's hoping it will lead you to a breakthrough! Take a moment to celebrate, reflect on what you've learned, and plan your next moonshot.

Next Steps

Looking for more? Go to our website at TheMoonshotGroup.com. There you'll find blog posts, videos, and more.

If you're interested in the resources we've mentioned in this book or want further reading on related topics, check the *Resources* section that follows.

66 The Moon is the first milestone on
the road to the stars. **99**

ARTHUR C. CLARKE,
SCIENCE FICTION AUTHOR

SOURCES AND RESOURCES

SOURCES ABOUT THE MOONSHOT

The NASA website is a rich source of information about everything related to the original Moonshot. We visited it repeatedly during the writing of this book.

You can find countless books on the Apollo program and the Moonshot. Here are a few that inspired and guided us:

- *Failure Is Not an Option: Mission Control From Mercury to Apollo 13 and Beyond*, by Gene Kranz (Simon & Schuster)

- *Moonfire: The Epic Journey of Apollo 11*, by Norman Mailer and Colum McCann (Taschen)

- *Marketing the Moon*, by David Meerman Scott and Richard Jurek (The MIT Press)

- *Team Moon: How 400,000 People Landed Apollo 11 on the Moon*, by Catherine Thimmesh (Houghton Mifflin Company)

The John F. Kennedy Presidential Library and Museum is a wonderful source of information on the Kennedy presidency, and worth a visit when in the Boston area.

OTHER SOURCES CITED IN THE BOOK

INTRODUCTION

The excerpts of President Kennedy's speeches in this chapter and throughout the book are available at the Kennedy Library and in NASA records.

CHAPTER 1: FROM THE MOON TO EARTH

The story of Paul O'Neill's speech to Alcoa investors is told in many places, including Charles Duhigg's excellent book *The Power of Habit*. This book is also the source of the quote about O'Neill's reaction to the death of one of the company's employees.

A profile of Jeffrey Immelt in *Vanity Fair*, June 30, 2006, offered the story of Immelt's critics from Fox News and the Green Party alike. Said Immelt, "I know I'm doing something right when I have the left saying it's not good enough and the right saying this is Communist corporate do-goodism bullshit." Find the article at http://www.vanityfair.com/news/2006/07/generalelectric200607.

CHAPTER 2: THE ESSENTIAL INGREDIENTS OF A MOONSHOT

Gene Kranz's book *Failure Is Not an Option* was the source for his quote in this chapter, and his quotes in other chapters.

The quote from Dr. Christopher Kraft comes from the NASA series of monographs on aerospace history, number 14: "Managing the Moon Program: Lessons Learned from Project Apollo."

The initial, cold reception of "Ecomagination" by GE's leadership was described in Bloomberg Business article "The Issue: Immelt's Unpopular Idea," by Douglas MacMillan on March 4, 2008.

The story of the triathlon comes directly from Lisa's experience and conversations with Ohashi and his team.

CHAPTER 3: **CHOOSE YOUR MOON**

The tale of the MOSH project at Nokia comes from Lisa's consulting practice, and from the authors' interviews with Lee Epting.

CHAPTER 4: **LIFTOFF**

The transcript of the Kennedy meeting cited in this chapter is available on the NASA history site: history.NASA.gov.

CHAPTER 8: *ENVISION THE FUTURE*

You can listen to a sound recording of Kennedy's address at Rice University from the website of the John F. Kennedy Presidential Library and Museum (www.jfklibrary.org). The museum displays include an edited version of his notes for the speech, along with the deviations he made when actually giving the address.

Kate witnessed the balsa wood model of the Palm PDA firsthand, in her role as an early member of the Palm management team.

As an avid student of how the brain works, Jeff Hawkins has since founded a machine intelligence company called Numeta, and the Redwood Neuroscience Institute.

Find more research from James Kouzes and Barry Posner at www.leadershipchallenge.com.

The data on Myers-Briggs personality frequency comes from the Myers-Briggs organization. Review the frequency of any personality type at www.myersbriggs.org.

Herminia Ibarra conducts research on women in leadership. For a discussion of this research on women and vision, see her article with Otilia Obodaru, "Women and the Vision Thing," in the January 2009 issue of the *Harvard Business Review*.

CHAPTER 9: SUIT UP

Gene Kranz's quote about Christopher Kraft comes from his book *Failure Is Not an Option*.

For discussions on the topic of power poses, see Amy Cuddy's TED talk "Your Body Language Shapes Who You Are" and Deborah Gruenfeld's video on Power and Influence on the Stanford Graduate School of Business YouTube Channel.

Victoria Brescoll's research can be found in the *Administrative Science Quarterly*, Winter 2012, in the article "Who Takes the Floor and Why: Gender, Power, and Volubility in Organizations."

Daniel Pink cited research about interrogative self-talk in his wonderful book *To Sell Is Human*. The original research is found in *Psychological Science*, volume 21, April 2010, in the article "Motivating Goal-Directed Behavior Through Introspective Self Talk" by authors Ibrahim Senay, Solores Albarracin, and Kenji Noguchi.

CHAPTER 10: SECURE AN EXPLICIT COMMITMENT

The quote from President Johnson is one of many stories in David Meerman Scott's book *Marketing the Moon*. The quote originates in an oral history in the Lyndon B. Johnson Presidential Library.

CHAPTER 11: MAINTAIN THE SUPPLY LINES

James Webb was a pivotal figure at NASA; a short biography can be found on the website of the NASA History Program Office.

For the research on taking time for reflection, see the article "The Remedy for Unproductive Busyness" by Francesca Gina and Bradley Staats in the *Harvard Business Review*, April 23, 2015. (HBR.org)

CHAPTER 12: THE POWER OF ACKNOWLEDGMENT

Adam Grant's book *Give and Take* is our source for the story of Frank Lloyd Wright and his apprentices.

For more on the Harris/Interact poll about leadership and acknowledgment, see the article "The Top Complaints from Employees About Their Leaders" by Lou Solomon, in the *Harvard Business Review* Online, June 24, 2015.

CHAPTER 13: ELEVATE YOUR PEOPLE SKILLS

NASA's Johnson Space Center publishes the transcripts from the Apollo 11 mission on its website.

Daniel Kahneman's book *Thinking Fast and Slow* is about the division between the two different ways of thinking and making decisions, and offers valuable insight for the world of business.

The research about body language and negotiation was described in the article "Chameleons Bake Bigger Pies and Take Bigger Pieces" by William W. Maddux, Elizabeth Mullen, and Adam D. Galinsky, published in the *Journal of Experimental Social Psychology* (Vol. 44, issue 2, March 2008).

CHAPTER 14: EXPAND YOUR IMPACT

Mark Granovetter has published research into networking; see his article "The Strength of Weak Ties" in the *American Journal of Sociology* (May 1973).

For more stories of master networkers, see the book *Business Brilliant: Surprising Lessons from the Greatest Self-Made Business Icons* by Lewis Schiff.

The idea of five-minute favors comes from Adam Grant's book *Give and Take*.

CHAPTER 15: BE A HERO-MAKER, NOT A HERO

The quote from Eugene Cernan is one of the stories in David Meerman Scott's book *Marketing the Moon*.

CHAPTER 22: DIFFICULT CONVERSATIONS

The research about avoiding difficult conversations comes from VitalSmarts® Research.

For a good article about Albert Mehrabian's research into body language communications, read "Is Nonverbal Communication a Numbers Game?" by Jeff Thompson on the *Psychology Today* blog, September 30, 2011.

CHAPTER 23: **FROM BREAKDOWN TO BREAKTHROUGH**

The quote from Paul O'Neill about creating a crisis comes from Reinhardt Krause's article "Alcoa's Paul O'Neill Relied on Analysis and Safety to Boost His Company to the Forefront" in *Investor's Business Daily,* May 21, 2001.

CHAPTER 24: **CULTIVATE BREAKTHROUGHS**

3M's lead user methodology for surgical draping was described in the *Harvard Business Review* article "Creating Breakthroughs at 3M" by Eric von Hippel, Stefan Thomke, and Mary Sonnack, in the September–October 1999 issue.

CHAPTER 25: **FROM ENTREPRENEUR TO LEADER**

Read more about the growth mind-set in Carol Dweck's excellent book *Mindset: The New Psychology of Success.*

CHAPTER 26: **THE LAUNCH TEAM**

Noam Wasserman's book *The Founder's Dilemma* includes a discussion about the people challenges of startups.

Larry Keyser's quote is from the Apollo Experience Report titled "The Role of Flight Mission Rules in Mission Preparation and Conduct," available on the NASA Technical Reports server.

CHAPTER 27: **MISSION RULES FOR STARTUPS**

The quote from Christopher Kraft comes from the NASA monograph "Managing the Moon Program: Lessons Learned from Project Apollo," available on the site Hisory.NASA.gov. This moderated discussion covers the specific management challenges of the Apollo program and is a fascinating read.

Ryan Engley, VP of Customer Success at Unbounce, shared his story about the dashboards in conversation with us. The company has described the physical implementation of the dashboard in its blog, in case you're interested in doing the same in your business.

The research about firefighters comes from the article "Eating Together at the Firehouse" by Kevin M. Kniffin, Brian Wansink, Carole M. Devine, and Jeffry Sobal, and was published in the journal *Human Performance* (Volume 28, Issues 4, 2015).

David Burkus's book *The Myths of Creativity* is the source of the quote about conflict and creativity; it's a good read for anyone interested in fostering an atmosphere of innovation.

The insight about teams doing better with a devil's advocate comes from research conducted by Lindy Greer of Stanford University, along with Ruchi Sinha of the University of South Australia, Niranjan Janardhanan of the University of Texas, Donald Conlon of Michigan State University, and Jeff Edwards of the University of North Carolina. Read the summary in the article "Do You Have a Contrarian on Your Team?" by Elizabeth MacBride on the Stanford Graduate School of Business Insights site, published November 13, 2015.

The story about constructive criticism at Pixar was described in David Burkus's book *The Myths of Creativity*.

CHAPTER 28: STARTUP STORIES

The quote from Lisa Suennen, a venture capital investor, comes from the article "6 Things You Need to Have in Your VC Pitch," published in *VentureBeat* on September 23, 2010.

Index

critical go/no-go, 127

defining, 124–26

examples of, 124, 125, 159–60

number of, 125

on-track or off-track reporting
for, 148–50, 238

for startups, 236–38

transforming missed, 164–65

working backward from
critical, 237–38

mirroring, 98–99, 102–3

mission creep, 160

mission rules
defining, 132–33
for startups, 217–26

momentum
building, 167
jump-starting, 128–29

Moonshot (original). *See also
individual space missions*
challenge of, 2
cost of, 67
initial reaction to, 20
long-term effects from, 3–4,
16–17, 34–35
milestones of, 124, 159–60
objective of, 12
opposition to, 12, 32, 77–78
scope of involvement in, 2
sources about, 253

moonshot effect
definition of, 5
examples of, 16–17

extent of, 33–36

primary spheres of, 7

reflecting on, 166–67

transformations through, 5, 6,
7, 35–36

moonshots (business)
abandoning, 180–81
building business case for,
44–45
challenge of, 15–16, 19, 21
definition of, 4–5
essential ingredients of, 19–22
examples of, 13–15
generating ideas for, 43–44
launch plan for, 41–47
in mature companies, 5
as noble pursuits, 16
publicity for, 29–30
resistance to, 30–32, 75–76
setting target for, 22, 25–28, 44
startups and, 5, 37–39
unexpected nature of, 19, 20
value of, 5–6, 20, 22, 33

Mueller, George, 95

Myers-Briggs, 53

N

NASA (National Aeronautics and
Space Administration).
*See also individual space
missions*

compressed timeline and, 129
critical go/no-go milestones
and, 127
milestones, defining, 124–26
within NASA, 123–24, 127
quick wins and, 128–29

Ritz-Carlton, 229–30

Rodriguez, Amy, 118

Rule of Three, 145–46

Rules of Engagement, 133–34,
225–26

R

Rapinoe, Megan, 118

rapport, building and
maintaining, 95–103

red binder effect, 158

reflection, scheduled, 84–85

requests
demands vs., 152
following up, 156–57
making effective, 153–55, 157
potential gaps and, 152–53
recording, 158
responses to, 155–56
startups and, 238–40

resets, 164–65

resilience, importance of, 204–5,
207

resistance, overcoming, 30–32

Rice University, 4, 51–52, 57

Ries, Eric, 204

right vs. effective, being, 116–19

risk taking, culture of, 221

S

Schiff, Lewis, 108

Siebel, Tom, 243

silence, 64, 175–76

simplicity, power of, 31

small talk, 102

Smith, Dylan, 207

Smylie, Ed, 182

"so that" technique, 85–86

startups. *See also* entrepreneurs
advisors for, 241–45
board of directors for, 247–49
causes of failure of, 211, 219
CEOs of, 206–9
clear requests and, 238–40
decision-making in, 202–3,
206
failure rate for, 191
founding stories of, 228
founding team of, 211–12
milestones and completions
for, 236–38
mission rules for, 217–26

moonshots and, 5, 37–39

organizational structure of, 213–14

problem solving and, 193–99

roles and responsibilities in, 214–15

Rules of Engagement in, 225–26

work environment of, 219–20, 222–23

stories

connecting personal, 101–2, 103

details of, 232

founding, 228

hero of, 232

importance of, 227

inviting new employees into, 233

structure of, 231–32

values, 229–30

war, 230–31

storytelling, 227–33

successes

celebrating, 159–67

envisioning, 56

Suennen, Lisa, 228

Ackowledgments

FROM LISA GOLDMAN & KATE PURMAL

The talents and support of a host of contributors made this project possible.

We acknowledge the immense contribution of Anne Janzer. She brilliantly lent her skill and insight to capture the essence of our message, built on it with her own ideas and research, and masterfully crafted it for our readers. Her prolific writing, collaboration, and support made this book into something much greater than we imagined possible.

We are indebted to other contributors who brought this project to fruition: Pamela Kim collected our early ideas and organized them into a coherent concept; Lee Caraher and Karen Kang shared their experiences in ways that allowed us to stand on their shoulders; Karla Olson's publishing genius guided us in a graceful set of business decisions; Jenn White-Topliff created a striking cover that captured our visual story; Charles McStravick crafted a compelling book design that brings elegance to the publication; the insights of Steve Almond and Mark Levy shaped our early drafts into a more compelling manuscript; Laurie Gibson and Lisa Wolff edited the book to connect effortlessly with the reader.

We are grateful to our clients and colleagues who have contributed to our work and careers, and formed the basis for the insights and practices presented in this book. Our work with them is a laboratory for observing their courage, fortitude, and skill in the face of the inspiring challenges they accept and meet daily.

We are especially indebted to Ann Acierno, Yuki Amemiya, Karen Appleton, Bill Bain, Elise Bauer, Rosemary Brisco, Matt Clark, Joe Cohen, Burt Cummings, Elaine Cummings, David-Michel Davies, Barry Eggers,

Thomas Enraght-Moony, Lee Epting, Dave Evans, Nate Evans, Peter Falzon, Lindy Greer, Itai Gurari, Scott Kim, Lisa Kristine, Doug Leeds, Alison Macondray, Liz McMillan, Meta Mehling, Zen Ohashi, Barbara Rice, Sara Roberts, Elana Rosen, Lisa Ross, Jose Solis, Sarah Tavel, Neil Vogel, Barry Waitte, Pam Wallack, and Karilee Wirthlin.

FROM LISA GOLDMAN

This book is dedicated to Howard Goldman, my husband and partner for over thirty years. His respect allows me to live fully in the world. His wisdom washes over everything he touches and makes it something previously unimagined. The vitality of my life and the dynamics nature of my consulting work are the true beneficiaries of his generous gifts.

I am the product of great teachers and mentors. My father, Sy Miller, remains for me an exemplar of practicing the highest and most compassionate values in business. My mother, Fran Miller, observed keenly and taught me to imbue people with generous purpose. My family—Rob Miller, Kelly Miller, Isabel Miller, Ivy Miller, Hazi Goldman, Christina Goldman, Rose Simon, Randy Simon, Sydney Tinkelman, and Carl Tinkelman—provide an environment where possibility and compassion flourish. I hope to live up to the values and attributes each of these people has conferred upon me.

My community of friendship is a source of inspiration and joy. I must single out Patty Leeper and Kimberly Jenkins, who renew that reservoir during our every interaction. Their deep friendship and connection has allowed me to call upon and develop strengths that have contributed immeasurably to this project. My network of relationships has been deep and dear to me; please forgive me if I have not cited you directly.

I am privileged to have created and benefited from my long-term professional partnership with Kate Purmal. Embarking on this project has called upon me to contribute in extraordinary ways that would not have been possible without Kate's sharp impetus. Her humor, keen sense of purpose, and complementary skill set contribute to outcomes I could not have imagined at the outset. I am ever thankful to Kate's collaboration, and for teaching me what it means to be fully engaged.

FROM KATE PURMAL

This book is dedicated to my children, Mariah and Cole Driver, who give me endless joy; and whose spirit, courage, brilliance, and determination inspire me to bring forth my best. And to my parents, Jean and Jerry Purmal, for their constant love and encouragement, and for instilling in me the belief that I could accomplish anything I set my mind to.

I am deeply grateful to Jennifer Hagan for her love and support, for inspiring me to tell stories, and for encouraging me to write and share ideas.

I am thankful for my family—Tony Purmal and Janett Peace, Tim and Tom Gundlach, Colin Purmal, and Ben and Daniel Gundlach—and to Brad Driver for always being there to raise our delightful children together.

My life is fueled by the love and support of my dear friends, especially Justine Rosenthal, who is always on the path beside me, and Kim Haddad, who has become the sister I always wanted.

I have had the privilege of working with extraordinary leaders who transformed the trajectory of my career: Eli Harari, Jeff Karan, Ed Colligan, Jeff Hawkins, Donna Dubinsky, Ken Dulaney, and Alan Lefkof. Thank you for believing in me and giving me opportunities to excel and lead.

When I became a CEO, the first person I called was Lisa Goldman. I knew that with her guidance and counsel I would succeed. Lisa's partnership has been the single most important of my career; together we've launched moonshots, run companies, served on boards, and advised clients. In the process we've built a lifelong friendship and created a deep well of mutual admiration and affection. Our work together on this book has been effortless and joyful. Thank you, Lisa. I cherish the hours we've spent together shaping ideas and creating magic.